SAINT AUGUSTINE'S

Memory

GARRY WILLS

SAINT AUGUSTINE'S
Memory

VIKING

VIKING
Published by the Penguin Group
Penguin Putnam Inc., 375 Hudson Street, New York, New York 10014, U.S.A.
Penguin Books Ltd, 80 Strand, London WC2R 0RL, England
Penguin Books Australia Ltd, 250 Camberwell Road,
Camberwell, Victoria 3124, Australia
Penguin Books Canada Ltd, 10 Alcorn Avenue, Toronto, Ontario, Canada M4V 3B2
Penguin Books India (P) Ltd, 11 Community Centre, Panchsheel Park,
New Delhi—110 017, India
Penguin Books (N.Z.) Ltd, Cnr Rosedale and Airborne Roads, Albany,
Auckland, New Zealand
Penguin Books (South Africa) (Pty) Ltd, 24 Sturdee Avenue, Rosebank,
Johannesburg 2196, South Africa

Penguin Books Ltd, Registered Offices:
Harmondsworth, Middlesex, England

First published in 2002 by Viking Penguin,
a member of Penguin Putnam Inc.

10 9 8 7 6 5 4 3 2 1

LIBRARY OF CONGRESS CATALOGING-IN-PUBLICATION DATA

Augustine, Saint, Bishop of Hippo.
    Saint Augustine's memory : / [introduction and
commentary by] Garry Wills.
        p. cm
    ISBN 0-670-03127-5 (alk. paper)
    1. Augustine, Saint, Bishop of Hippo. 2. Christian saints—Algeria—Hippo
(Extinct city)—Biography. I. Wills, Garry, 1934– II. Title.

BR65.A6 E5 2002
270.2'092—dc21   2002019841
[B]

This book is printed on acid-free paper. ♾

Printed in the United States of America
Set in Aldus with Phaistos display and MT Arabesque Ornaments
Designed by Carla Bolte

TO JAMES O'DONNELL

sine quo non

CONTENTS

Key to Brief Citations   ix
Foreword   xi

PART I. INTRODUCTION: THE BOOK
OF MEMORY 1

1. *Memory as Dynamic*   4
2. *Memory as Constructive*   10
3. *Memory as the Self*   11
4. *Memory as Guide to Conduct*   14
5. *Memory as the Basis of Community*   18
6. *The Pathos of Memory*   20
7. *God in Memory*   22
8. *Memory in Book Ten of* The Testimony   26

PART II. *THE TESTIMONY,* BOOK TEN 27

I. WHY SHOULD OTHERS OVERHEAR ME?   29

II. THE CURRENT SEARCH FOR GOD   41

III. THE CONTENTS OF MEMORY   49
1. *Representations* (imagines)   49
2. *Rules* (percepta)   55
3. *Axioms* (rationes)   61
4. *Reactions* (affectiones)   63
5. *Forgetting* (oblivio)   69
6. *Happiness* (beata vita)   77
7. *God* (Deus)   89

IV. THE FLESH'S URGES   93
    1. The Five Senses: Touch   95
    2. The Five Senses: Taste   99
    3. The Five Senses: Smell   105
    4. The Five Senses: Hearing   107
    5. The Five Senses: Sight   109

V. TRANSGRESSIVE KNOWLEDGE
(*curiositas*)   117

VI. WORLDLY DESIGNS   125

VII. CONCLUSION   135

PART III.   COMMENTARY 145

PART IV.   APPENDIX:
    THE TESTIMONY, BOOK ELEVEN . . . 191

PART V.   LIST OF BASIC TERMS 225

Key to Brief Citations

Boldface numerals in square brackets **[1]** refer to paragraphs in Book Ten of *The Testimony*.

comm. refers to the Commentary on Book Ten (pp. 145).

O, with volume and page (e.g., O 3.225), refers to James J. O'Donnell, *Augustine "Confessions"* (Oxford, 1992).

T, with book and paragraph number (e.g., T 11.20), refers to the books of *The Testimony* other than Book Ten.

terms refers to Part V, List of Basic Terms.

I translate all Scripture texts from the Latin versions Augustine used. The Psalms are numbered as in the Vulgate Bible and in the Douay-Rheims Catholic translation of them.

FOREWORD

Augustine's *Testimony* (*Confessiones*) is written in thirteen books. Book Ten is the hinge book, making the turn between an account of God's graces shown to Augustine before his baptism (Books One through Nine) and a meditation on his life as baptized into the Trinity (Books Eleven through Thirteen). This makes Book Ten the key to the whole, and it contains his treatment of the work's central concept, memory. That concept is central not merely because he had to remember his past in order to give the account in the first nine books, but because memory is the place where he meets God and others—and himself. Memory bears a greater weight of meaning in his work than in that of any other major thinker. This is true not only of *The Testimony* but of his other books as well—especially *The Trinity*, where memory is the analogue in humans of God the Father, the *creating* deity.

Although Book Ten is the principal source for Augustine's treatment of memory (it takes up over half the book), this treatment is closely associated with his thought on time, which takes up almost the whole of Book Eleven. Since I cite Book Eleven often in my Introduction and Commentary, and since Book Eleven is only about half the length of Book Ten, I append a new translation of Book Eleven so that my references to it can be checked in their context.

I should say a word at the start about the place of *The Testimony* in Augustine's life. That life straddles the fourth and fifth centuries. He was born in North Africa (modern Algeria) at the middle of the fourth century (354) and he completed *The Testimony* just before the beginning of the fifth century. His formative years had occurred by then—he was baptized in 387, ordained a priest in 391, and consecrated a bishop in 396. He had taken his one trip out of Africa (383–387), and he was settling in for a third of a century serving as Bishop of Hippo. Before the new century began, he decided to take stock of his life, in his mid-forties, creating a book with the form of an intimate prayer to God. Up to this point, his longer works had been mainly polemical engagements with African schismatics (Donatists) and empire-wide heretics (Manichaeans). After 400, he would write his long works on broader subjects: *First Meanings in Genesis, The Trinity, The City of God*. This great change in his life was signaled and partly achieved by *The Testimony*, in which he went deep into himself in order to emerge as the visionary for others on a larger public stage. It was all a drama prepared in the depths of his own memory.

PART I

Introduction: The Book of Memory

A friend of mine says he finds Augustine's stress on memory a great disappointment. It seems to orient the Bishop of Hippo toward his own past, while my friend looks to the future—he calls himself a progressive, and Augustine a nostalgist. That friend, I am sure, speaks for many. We tend to be critical of people "living in the past," who are by definition conservative or reactionary. They have closed off new ideas in order to fondle previously experienced (or imagined) glories. America, by contrast, is thought of as a country that has rejected the past and turned confidently to a future that will be greater than anything that went before.

A first impression of Augustine's Book Ten might be taken as confirmation of this judgment against memory. He introduces the subject with a venture into memory as a huge warehouse, the storage place of old experiences, a passive place of deposit, a kind of glorified dump. The imagery at times is of a filing system slightly jumbled, where pieces may be out of order but are nonetheless static things being slotted into stable repositories, "everything ticketed [*commendatum*] here and stored for preservation" **[12]**. "Here all these things are stored, individually and by type, according to their means of accession . . . all received for deposit in or withdrawal from memory's huge vault" **[13]**. But these passing references, suggestive of a mental filing system, are belied in the general treatment of Augustine's memory. This memory is dynamic, constructive, predictive, constitutive of identity, the meeting place with other humans, and the pathway to God.

1. Memory as Dynamic

The interior that Augustine describes is far from having the air of an office or warehouse. Its "internal scenery" fluctuates as eerily as the landscape in Winsor McCay's *Little Nemo* comic strips.

> The scope of memory is vast, my God, in some way scary, with its depths, its endless adaptabilities—yet what are they but my own mind, my self? Then what can that self be, my God? What is my makeup? A divided one, shifting, fierce in scale. In memory alone there are uncountable expanses, hollows, caverns uncountably filled with uncountable things of all types **[26]**.

This is a place that recedes as he proceeds into it **[65]**. "I rummage through all these things, darting this way and that, plunging down as far as I can go, and reaching no bottom" **[26]**. It is a "terrain of trouble" **[14]**. He bumps into himself in this scenery **[14]**. His inner self, dwarfed by the mountains and star systems held in memory, has inner eyes and ears, even an inner hand **[12]**, a mental mouth and stomach **[22]**. Augustine's inner Nemo crawls about in perilous situations that recall Gerard Manley Hopkins's sonnet "No Worst":

> O the mind, mind has mountains; cliffs of fall
> Frightful, sheer, no-man-fathomed. Hold them cheap
> May who ne'er hung there.

The memories themselves are in motion, eluding him, flying in his face unbidden, like bats in a cave: "Jumbled memories flirt out on their own, interrupting the search for what I want" **[12]**. Laboriously pieced-together concepts deliquesce and must be reassembled:

> [I]f I forgo their retrieval, even for brief intervals, they sink out of sight again, sliding deep into some inner windings, and they must be pressed up out of that place (for where else could they have gone?) and pressed again into knowable form. We must, that is, reconnect them after their dispersion **[18]**.

The things deposited in memory do not just lie there passively. When they are not disintegrating from neglect, they are being reshaped by each recurrence to them. The Augustine remembering is different from the one who remembered any matter in the first place, or re-remembered in preceding recurrences to it; and the matter itself is being altered by cognate things all around it. Here, for instance, Augustine discusses the immutable truths of the numerical sciences:

> All these things I not only remember but remember learning them. And many arguments against them I remember hearing; and however false the arguments may be, my memories of hearing them are not false. And I remember distinguishing between what was true and what was said against the truth—an

act of distinguishing I remember one way now, which is different from the way I remember often going over the distinction while I was expressing it. I remember these frequent acts from the past, and what I distinguish and conclude now I am laying away in memory, so I can remember in the future what I concluded at this moment. So, just as I have a memory of past remembering, so in the future, if I recall what I conclude now, I shall be recalling it by the power of memory [20].

Remembering is a process that never rests. Things can never be fixed in memory—and no wonder: they were not fixed in the original experience that is being remembered. That too, was a process, one that Augustine considers in Book Eleven's treatment of time. If you commit a sentence to memory, it is not acquired as a single thing and then turned over intact to memory. When you pronounce the second word of the sentence, you are already remembering the first one, which is now in the past. Unless you remember it you cannot tell what the subject is or how the sentence should end. And so with each word, and each element of sound in each word.

If we suppose some particle of time which could not be divided into a smaller particle, that alone deserves to be called the present. Yet it flies in so headlong a way out of the future and into the past that no slightest moment of rest can reach itself out in pause. If it paused, its earlier part could be divided from its later. Thus the present itself has no length (T 11.20).

This process leaves a representation (*imago*) of itself in the mind, and that is what enters the memory. It is sufficiently detached from its cause to be recalled in isolation from the original experience. Yet it involves a kind of reliving of that experience, which was a temporal event, involving succession to reach completion. *Imago* in this context is usually translated (or transliterated) as "image," which gives a misleading suggestion that the sense-experience prints a facsimile in the mind, of the seal-in-wax sort. But Augustine remembers states and conditions that are temporally articulated and would not leave a single imprint. He speaks, for instance, of remembering happiness, his boyhood, health, sickness, and emotional reactions like fear and desire, and complicated historical developments. I choose the term "re-presentation" because the remembering is for him a literal re-presentizing, a living through again of what was a *process* at every stage of the mind's engagement. In fact, he argues that the past no longer exists except in representations of it in our minds. And that representation is always a present one when we have recourse to it. He would agree with the saying "The past is not dead, it is not even past."

What should be clear and obvious by now is that we cannot properly say that the future or the past exists, or that there are three times, past, present, and future. Perhaps we can say that there are three tenses, but that they are the present of the past, the present of the present, and the present of the future. This would correspond, in some sense, with a triad I find in the soul and nowhere else, where the past is present to memory, the present is present to observation [*contuitus*], and the future is present to anticipation (T 11.26).

The past, therefore, is not an inert structure in which we can deposit a remembered item to remain unchanged until called up again. The original experience must be re-presentized by a rememberer, with all the accumulated alterations in that rememberer since his last encounter with the memory—with, perhaps, new insights, or with deeper prejudices. And the thing remembered is as charged with emotional content as is the person remembering. In fact, what is being recalled is the *experience* that a person underwent in acquiring anything to be remembered. That is why conditions that surrounded the first acquirement come along with it, or even precede it—which is Proust's madeleine effect. Augustine instructs his own mind on this point:

> So time is measured, my mind, in you. Raise no clamor against me—I mean against yourself—out of your jostling reactions [*affectiones*]. I measure time in you, I tell you, *because* I measure the reactions that things caused in you by their passage, reactions that remain when the things that occasioned them have passed on (T 11.36).

Affectiones in that passage is often translated "emotions" or "impressions," but those words give a wrong impression if they imply that an *ad-fectio* is something done to a a soul by the impact of other things on it. For Augustine the soul is always active. It "goes out" through the senses to apprehend things, for instance. It reacts to occasions given it (to learn, to feel, to accept, to reject), but the stimulation or provocation just calls up the soul's own action. So, in remembering, the soul actively relives its putting together of future and past in the first place.

This concept of the memory as a reliving of original experience helps Augustine with the mysterious fact that he remembers forgetting things. "What can forgetting be but a lack of memory? And then how can forgetting be present, for me to remember it, when its very presence makes me lack it?" [24]. Some sense of the *process* involved in the lost memory's acquisition or retention may persist as a kinetic tilt in the mind's motion, "as if the memory had some feeling that it was not moving with something it had moved with before, but was limping, as it were, from the lack of what it was used to, and trying to recover what was missing" [28]. What is important, and characteristic, is that Augustine thinks in dynamic terms, as if going through the *motion* of a memory would revive it—his way of eating the madeleine to find what it will bring back.

This dynamic view of memory can be read, today, as a destabilizing of memory. It certainly fits in with modern research that finds memory "unreliable." In popular usage we still distinguish between one who is "really" remembering and one who is fabricating. But for Augustine, all memory is fabrication—that is one of its glories.

2. *Memory as Constructive*

We have seen that for Augustine any experience must already be constructed for it to be made available to memory. That is, we must remember the first part of a sentence in order to complete the sentence. That putting together of something in the fleeting "present" involves the mind's double reach (*distentio*) to become the medium of transit from the future into the past. Since we cannot really "live in the present"—in a fleeting unfixed moment between what is future and what is past—all our thought must use the materials supplied to it by memory. By manipulation of those materials we develop our concepts. Even abstract concepts, not drawn directly from memory of the senses' information, have to be built up from things already supplied in memory:

> We can conclude, then, that to learn these things—those, namely, whose representations are not pulled into us through the senses, but directly perceived, in and for themselves inside us, with no aid at all from the senses—is to express in a connected way what was latent in the memory (but scattered about in disorder), and to make deliberate provision for their manageable arrangement (so that the scattered and disordered elements are reduced to a state readily accessed for the mind's use) **[18]**.

In *The Teacher*, Augustine told his son that no one teaches us language. He felt, like Noam Chomsky, that the rules of language are inborn. But memory is necessary to supply the agreed-upon symbols for things that give any specific language its vocabulary.

> All by myself [as an infant], using the brain you gave me, my God . . . I began to *use my memory* to pull in what I desired. Whenever people named something, and used the same inflections when indicating that thing with their bodies, I would take note and store *in memory* the fact that they made the same sound when they wanted to indicate that thing. . . . The words I heard, used in their right way in different grammatical settings, and recurring over time, I steadily accumulated and, wrestling my mouth around those sounds, I expressed what I wanted (T 1.13, emphasis added).

The idea that living in memory binds one to a dead past assumes that the things in memory are unchanging and limited to their content at the point of their original acquisition. But Augustine saw memory as a laboratory in which we are continually refashioning everything we remember—which is everything we know. We even remake ourselves in that crucible.

3. Memory as the Self

Without memory we would have no sense of our own identity. That is the point of all the stories about amnesiacs. To wake with no memory of who one is, what one has done, what one's relations to others are, is to be denuded of one's very nature, since that depends on maintaining a continuity with one's former actions. A symbol of the amnesiac curse is given in Milan Kundera's novel *The Unbearable Lightness of Being*. People trying to disorient the Soviet invaders of Prague tear down street signs—only to find themselves disoriented when the occupation is over, and street directions are forgotten by some residents of Prague, taking away neighborhood memories and community associations.

Modern stories of amnesia assume that its victim is stranded in a present without a past—that such a person "has no memory." Since Augustine holds that there is no real present, the person waking with amnesia would have a memory, but it would be of the first instant that passed. Having said "I," the person will remember that subject and feel the agony of being unable to connect it with a predicate. This would be a concrete instance of his "remembering that I forget." Memory, the forge of identity, becomes a torture of deprivation.

An undamaged memory supplies us with endless predicates for our subject "I." Some of them are disconcerting, some reassuring. We remember our sinning self, but also remember our loves given and received. We have an observed as well as an observing self. In that sense, memory first alienates us from ourselves in order to make it possible for us to reclaim ourselves. As Augustine puts it: "[T]his is where I bump up against myself, when I call back what I did, and where, and when, and how I felt when I was doing it" **[14]**. This mystery of being both the observer-I and observed-I was very suggestive to

Augustine—he would find in it a trace of the way God is "in God's company" (John 1.1) in the Trinity.

How do we think about ourselves? When we think of something else, we put it before our gaze, actually or mentally. We move it from a place of concealment or neglect into a place for viewing. But how can we do that for ourselves?

> When the mind sets itself before itself to express what it sees, does the mind see part of itself with some other part of itself as we see parts of our body with another part of it, the eyes, by putting those parts in the eyes' line of sight? Who could say or think anything sillier? Where would we bring the mind from, to put it in its own line of sight, except from itself? And where would we take it for viewing except in front of itself? Will it, then, no longer be where it was, before it was moved into the line of sight, since moving it there means removing it from somewhere? And if it is moved out in front of itself to be seen, what position will it maintain to do the seeing? Does it become its own twin, as it were, one staying here in order to do the viewing, the other moving there in order to be viewed, so it can be inside itself when seeing and in front of itself when seen? (*The Trinity* 14.9).

Augustine quickly rebukes himself for thinking of the mind in physical terms; but he says he uses such imagery to point out that there is some kind of alienation from the self involved in grasping the self: "When the mind wants to express itself, it recollects itself by a kind of immaterial turning back upon itself" (ibid). He puts the matter even more vividly in *The*

Testimony (8.16): "While he [Pontician] was speaking, Lord, you twisted me back upon myself, dragging me out from behind my own back, where I had cowered to avoid seeing myself, and planted me before my own gaze, where I might see the foul me." We can hide from ourselves in memory, as well as find ourselves there. We can disguise ourselves, lurk in shadows, or wear masks. But whether we meet the real self or a falsified one, there is nowhere we can go for the encounter but into our own memory.

4. Memory as Guide to Conduct

Since the future is unknown and not directly knowable, while the present is a fleeting instant that cannot be fixed in order to make it serve as our guide, our future actions must be based on what is in the memory, not as isolated items, unchanging and unconnected, but as chains of past consequence whose trajectory can be projected into the future. In that sense, we all drive forward by looking into our rearview mirror.

> From this store of things there are new and ever newer representations of my experiences, or of things accepted in the past on the basis of trust. These I recombine with representations of the past to ponder future actions, their consequences and possibilities, all considered (once more) as present. Within that vast inner chamber of my mind, stocked with representations of so great number and so great variety, I say to myself: This I shall

do, or that—and this will follow, or that will. I say to myself: If only this would happen, or that would! Or: God keep me from this, or from that. And the minute I say it, from that vast treasure store of memory the representations of what I am describing [as in the future] are supplied at once—I could not say any of these things if the representations were not available to me **[14]**.

The mind is trafficking here in what Augustine calls the three presents—the present of the past, the present of the present, and the present of the future (recollection, observation, anticipation)—in a series of stages: a) forming new and ever-newer representations of things by combining prior materials, then b) recombining (literally "weaving into," *contexo*) these newly formed representations with old ones, then c) weighing various chains of action in the broad range of possibilities now available to the mind.

In Book Eleven Augustine addresses even more directly the problem of knowing the future. He says we must surmise where we cannot know, on the basis of past connections.

So when some are said to foretell the future, they are not seeing the future, which does not yet exist, because it is still to come—perhaps they see some preconditions or indications of the future, which do exist already. So to them the objects of their prediction are not future but present; they are materials from which the mind can form estimates of what will be. These estimates, too, are in the present, and those predicting the future are actually seeing their own present estimates.

From many possible examples of this, I cite one. Looking at

the morning twilight, I predict that the sun will rise. What I see is present, what I foresee is future—not that the sun will exist (it already does), but that its rise will exist. That has not yet occurred, so I could not predict its rise without having an image of that event in my mind (as I do even now when I mention it). Two things I see—the twilight preceding sunrise, which yet is not sunrise, and the image of sunrise in my mind, which is also not sunrise. Both these things must be seen in the present for the future to be predicted—the sun's rising. Future things are not yet. And if not yet, then not at all. And if they are not at all, they cannot be seen. But they can be predicted from things which already are, and are already seen (T 11.24).

Memory—not of one sunrise, but of repeated sunrises, and memory of linking these into patterns of expectable recurrence— makes safe projections possible. Without those past patterns existing in the memory, no expectation of sunrise could be based on a sound hypothesis. In that sense, the past gives birth to the future. Memory is the only solid basis for planning what we should do.

After reading Augustine one can only wonder what people think they are relying on when they say they do *not* need any remembered past to make decisions or plan the future. What other source do they have to supply them with their materials? Even the most futurist planners of utopias have used select elements of the past to create their (often thin and unrealistic) utopias. Most likely the claim to be totally independent of the past means that a person emphatically rejects some common version of the past and turns quietly, perhaps semiconsciously, to some more esoteric tradition. There is a certain amount of self-deception in this. Refusal to face the great mass of past experience can lead to a cultism of the less apparent, making the result too unworldly to stand the buffetings of reality. As Gilbert Chesterton wrote in the *Daily News* for December 7, 1907:

Man is like Perseus; he cannot look at the Gorgon of the future except in the mirror of the past. All those who have tried to look at a fixed future directly have been turned to stone. The human heart has been petrified in them. . . . It is utterly useless to talk about enlarging one's mind with visions of the future. The future doesn't enlarge one's mind in the least. The future is a blank wall on which I can paint my own portrait as large as I like. If I am narrow, I can make the future narrow; if I am mean, I can make the future mean. I cannot make the past mean. I cannot make St. Catherine of Siena mean. I cannot make Plato narrow. In the past I have real antagonists, men certainly better, braver, or more brilliant than I. Among the dead I have living rivals. In the future all my rivals are dead because they are unborn. I know I could not write *Paradise Lost*, but I could easily write a Utopia very favorable to the sort of poetry I can write. . . . We are attracted to the future because it is what is called a soft job. In front of us lies an unknown or unreal world which we can mould according to every cowardice or triviality in our own temperament. But if we look back at our fathers, as they gather in the gate of history, we see it like the gate of Eden, described by one of them in verse which we cannot imitate: "With dreadful faces thronged and fiery arms."

Memory is broadening. It liberates us from the provincialism of the future.

5. Memory as the Basis of Community

We meet not only ourselves but others in memory. In amnesiac stories, the person afflicted with memory loss does not know whether he or she is married, or to whom. Who the person's parents might be, or children (if any), or partners, or foes—all those things are wiped out if the memory is gone. (This is the tragedy of advanced Alzheimer's disease, with grieving relatives no longer recognized by their loved one.) Community is built up on associations treasured in memory. Augustine formed his ideal of life in the brotherhood of his monastery from the intellectual friendships he formed with fellow graduate students in Carthage. Memory is not *only* nostalgia, but it can be that (among many other things), and nostalgia need not be escapist. It can be constructive.

Their qualities compelled my heart—conversation and laughter and mutual deferrings; shared readings of sweetly phrased books; facetiousness alternating with things serious; heated arguing (as if with oneself) to spice our general agreement with dissent; teaching and being taught by turns; the sadness at any-one's absence, and the joy of return. Reciprocated love uses such semaphorings—a smile, a glance, a thousand winning acts—to fuse separate souls into a single glow, no longer many souls but one (T 4.17).

It was mentioned earlier that Augustine learned to talk by taking overheard words into his memory. He also remembers how the supportive company of his nurses and family helped him acquire words from them, giving the Latin language warm communal associations (by contrast with his resistance to the harsh teachers trying to beat Greek into him). "I applied myself to learning them [Latin words], without intimidation or coercion, surrounded as I was by nurses who coaxed, adults who laughed, and others fond of playing with a child" (T 1.23). As a bishop, Augustine told his priests that they would teach others better by creating an atmosphere of love around their lessons. They would also learn while teaching in friendship: "The more, by the bond of love, we enter into each other's mind, the more even old things become new for us again" (*Christian Culture* 17). Modern studies of criminal behavior show that social deviants often lack memories of supportive family or other groups. Unable to meet such friends in their memories of the past, they find it difficult or impossible to form friends in the present. Memory is our path to others.

6. The Pathos of Memory

Augustine stresses the marvels of memory, of the mystery that is within him and that he is. But he also recognizes that memory is formed by a process of transit—from a future that is not yet, to a past that is no longer—that makes it radically contingent and labile. The very reach of the mind that makes the transit of things into memory involves a kind of dislocating wrench.

> Say I am about to recite a psalm I am familiar with. Before I start, my anticipation reaches [*tenditur*] to include the psalm in its entirety, but as I recite it, my memory reaches [*tenditur*] to take into the past each thing I shall be cropping from the future; so my soul's life-force [*vita hujus actionis meae*] reaches in opposite directions [*dis-tenditur*]—into memory by what I have just said, into anticipation for what I am about to say—while simultaneously reaching out [with *ad-tentio*] to the present through which what was future is being shuttled into what is past (T 11.38).

The verb *distenditur* is often translated "is extended" or "is stretched." But the wrenching *dis* (two-ways) is rightly emphasized by O'Donnell (O 3.289). The soul is always an *active* agent in Augustine, and a middle sense fits better with the cognate words used when this process is being described (*tenditur, attentio, intentio, extentio*). Besides, the soul partly transcends time by its reach, allowing it to stand above periods of time in such a way that it can compare their durations. But this partial transcendence, involving a resemblance to God, just makes more poignant the imprisonment in time that every human being must feel. The soul straddling the passage between future and past is *working* at its "reach in opposite directions." Augustine would like to repose in the glimpses he has been given of God's peace, glimpses swept away by the ruthless advance of time. He would say with Goethe's Faust (11582), "So beautiful! Stay on!"—but he is dissipated out from his own center in the endless shuttling of time through a mind unable to pause or have peace.

Since 'your pity superintends men's various lives,' behold how my life-force reaches in opposite directions. 'Your Right Hand has upheld me' in my Lord, the son of man, who mediates between your unity and our multiplicity (for we are multitudinous amid multitudinous things). Through him may I 'lay hold on him who has laid hold on me,' and be gathered out of my useless years by following the One, 'oblivious of the past,' not caring for future things that pass away but 'for things prior to them.' No longer reaching in opposite directions [*distentus*] but reaching forward [*extentus*] only—not with divided reach [*distentionem*] but with focused reach [*intentionem*]—'I seek the prize of your high calling,' where I may 'hear the song of praise' and 'contemplate your delight,' a thing not of the future or the past. But for now 'my years are passing amid sobs,' with only you to solace them, Lord, my everlasting father. I, however, have been disarticulated into time [*at ego in tempora dissilui*], I cannot put the times together in my mind, my very

> thoughts are shredded, my soul unstrung—till I flow together
> into you, purified, to melt into the fires of your love (T 11.39).

Because of his disarticulation into time, Augustine's memory is
full of failure and loss, and he must anticipate more temporal
troubles. Yet the yearning to melt into the still fires of God is
also a part of that memory, telling him of God as well as of
himself.

7. God in Memory

If memory is where Augustine meets himself and others, it is
also where he finds God.

> See what a long ramble I have made through my own memory,
> in quest of you, Lord, and I have not found you anywhere but
> inside it. Nothing about you have I found but what I remember
> from the time I began learning about you. . . . In my memory,
> then, you have been lodged from the time I first learned of you,
> and there I find you when I remember you and 'take delight in
> you' [35].

He learned about God from the preachers of the gospel, from
Scripture, and from the inner light (*illuminatio*) given him.
But he also learns from himself, since even with all man's
imperfections, the human person is the thing in all of earthly
creation that most resembles God: "Our mind cannot be understood, even by itself, because it is made in God's image" (*Ser-*

mon 398.2). The three presents of the soul are themselves a trace of the three persons in God. They transcend the past and future insofar as they are all an interwoven present, like the eternity of God's existence outside time. Human memory (the present of the past) is an image of the Father, who comes to know himself in himself, generating the other persons; he is the creator—as memory is where we come to know ourselves, and where we "create" all the "new and newer representations of things" by which we connect ourselves to the world God made. The reach out to the present of the present is an image of the Son, the Word of God, which articulates the transition from eternity to time, mediating between God and man. And the present of the future reflects the Holy Spirit, the Advocate who will come to complete the mission of the Son, bringing love's plan to its completion.

From the first paragraph of *The Testimony*'s first book, the pervasive reflection of the Trinity has been found in all of creation, according to a favorite text of Augustine: "You have ordered all things by measure (*mensura*) and number (*numerus*) and weight (*pondus*)" (Wisdom 11.21). The Father lays the architectonic foundation of the universe. The Son as Word articulates the separate wonders of the creation. And the Spirit acts by the weight of love (*amor meus, pondus meum,* T 13.10). In *The Trinity* (10.18), begun while he was polishing *The Testimony*, the Trinitarian structure of the human soul is spelled out as an interpenetration of the equal-and-distinctive memory (Father), understanding (Son), and will (Spirit).

These three things—memory, understanding, and will—are not three lives but one life, not three minds but one mind, and therefore not three substances but one substance.

Memory, for instance, when it is called life or mind, or substance, is being identified as separate to itself. But when it is called remember*ing* there is reference to something beyond itself [that is remembered].

The same holds true for understanding and willing. When called by those names, there is reference to something beyond themselves [to be understood or willed]. But each of them is, in itself, a life or mind or substance.

So all three are one, insofar as they share one life, one mind, one substance; and whenever they are named as such, the *singular*, not the plural, is to be used of each of them, and of all together. But they are a plural, three, when each refers, beyond itself, to the others.

And each is equal to the others, taken singly or together, since each *contains* the others, either singly or together. In fact, not only does each contain the others, but each contains the totality of all three.

For I *remember* that I have memory, understanding, and will.

I *understand* that I have understanding, and memory, and will.

I *will* that I will, and remember, and understand.

And I remember *all* of my memory and understanding and will, all at the same time. If there is any memory I do not remember, it is not in my memory; for nothing can be more remembered than what is in the memory. Thus my memory is of my *entire* memory.

Similarly, I know that I understand all that is in my understanding, and know that I will all that is in my will—and this knowledge, too, I remember.

I remember, then, the entirety of what I understand and what I will; and when I understand all three together, it is their entirety I understand. For when I do not know things that can be understood, they are not in my understanding. And what is outside my understanding I can neither remember nor will, since if I remember to will something understandable, it must be in my understanding.

My will, in the same way, contains the entirety of what I understand and what I remember, whenever I want to activate anything from my store of understanding or memory.

Since any of the three contains any of the other two, or all of them, they must be equal to any of the others, or to all of them, each to all and all to each—yet these three are one life, one mind, one substance.

There can be no higher compliment to human memory than to compare it to God the Father. To live in memory, then, is not to "live in the past," but to come near to the Beginning, the *origo,* in which God created all things and found them good.

8. *Memory in Book Ten of* The Testimony

Though the treatment of memory takes up over half of Book Ten, it subserves that book's main function, which is to mediate between the narrative of Augustine's life up to his baptism (Books One through Nine) and the contemplation of the role of the Trinity in that life (Books Eleven through Thirteen). Augustine responds here to those who ask not only how he was brought to the church but how he exists in it now. Since Augustine does not think there is a stable moment that can be called "the present," a description of his current state entails the ten years or so since his baptism. He must go into his memory to give this account. But beyond that he wants to tell us how he is seeking God, and that quest begins in memory, where alone he finds God. By seeking to purify his life he hopes to mount toward God, to study the mystery of the Trinity—the project of the final three books of *The Testimony*.

PART II

The Testimony, Book Ten

Notes

L1 *to know]* 1 Corinthians 13.12: "then I shall know, even as I am known."

L2 *invigorator]* *Virtus*—which gives life to the soul, as the soul gives life to the body.

L4 *blemish]* Ephesians 5.27 (of the church): "without blemish or wrinkle."

L5 *glad]* Romans 12.12: "being glad in hope."

L8 *truth . . . loved]* Psalm 50.8: "See, you have loved the truth."

L8 *enacts truth]* John 3.21: "the one who enacts truth comes to the light."

L13 *inmost depths]* Ecclesiasticus 41.18: "the inmost depths [*abyssum*] and heart of men he has scrutinized."

L20 *perspicuous]* 2 Corinthians 5.11: "but to God we are perspicuous [*manifesti*]."

I. Why Should Others Overhear Me?

1.   You, who know me, may I come 'to know, even as I am known.' Enter into my soul, you its invigorator, and make it capable of you, so that you can retain and maintain it 'without blemish or wrinkle.' This is my hope, my reason for speaking to you, 'glad in hope' when I am rightly glad. As for other things in life, apart from this, the only lamentable thing is lamenting their loss, or rather *not* to lament lamenting them. For 'truth is what you have loved,' and 'whoever enacts truth comes to the light.' I want to enact the truth—before you, by my testimony; and, by my writing, before those who bear witness to this testimony.

2.   Were I not to offer this testimony to you, what would I be hiding from you, since 'the inmost depths' of human awareness lie exposed to your view? I would be sealing you off from me, not me from you. Instead of that, my sobs are a warrant against any satisfaction taken in myself, and you shine into me, soothe me, make yourself loved by me and longed for, so that I, an embarrassment to myself, abandon me and turn to you, finding no way to satisfy myself or you but in you. I, whatever I may be, 'am perspicuous to you.' My motive in testifying I have declared, and its means are not physical words the body utters, but words the spirit utters, for you hear the mind crying

L3 *bless the just]*   Psalm 5.13: "for you bless the just."

L3 *make him just]*   Romans 4.5: "for one believing in him who makes the wicked just."

L4 *to your view]*   Psalm 95.6: "Testimony and beauty are before his view." The picture is of a criminal before the judge, unable to speak because of his guilt.

L10 *treat my symptoms]*   Psalm 102.3: "you who treat all my symptoms [*languores*—see *terms*]."

L10 *transgressive knowledge]*   See *terms* for *curiositas*.

L15 *no man knows]*   1 Corinthians 2.11: "Who knows what is within except a man's own spirit, which is within?"

L21 *love is all-believing]*   1 Corinthians 13.7: "love is all-believing."

L22 *union to love]*   Ephesians 4.2–4: "supporting each other in love, careful to keep the spirit's unity in a bond of peace, one body and one spirit."

L23 *shall risk]*   *Etiam sic,* literally "even under such conditions."

out to you. The testimony to my sin is simply my anguish at it, as my testimony to any good I do is simply not taking credit for it, since you, Lord, 'bless the just man,' but first you 'make him just.' Tacit, then, is the testimony I offer 'to your view'—yet not so. It is tacit in sound but clamorous in emotion. Nor can I say anything worthwhile to others that you did not hear from me first, any more than you can hear me say anything to you that you did not first say to me.

3.   But why let others overhear my testimony, as if they could treat my symptoms? People want a transgressive knowledge of others' lives, but are blissfully ignorant of what might change their own. Why, anyway, should they care to hear from me about my own condition if they will not hear from you about theirs? If they hear me describing myself, how can they know whether I am telling the truth (since 'no man knows what is within but a man's own spirit, which is also within him'); but if they are listening to you about their own condition, what can they say—that the Lord is lying to them? Is there, in fact, any way they can learn about themselves *except* by listening to you? Whoever calls what he learns from you a lie is lying to himself. Yet since 'love is all-believing'—for those, at least, united to others by their 'union to love itself'— I shall risk testifying to you, Lord, in such a way that, even though I cannot be the one to make my own testimony credible to others, the love with which they listen will lend it credit.

4.   Clarify for me, you who medicine my inmost self, my motive in continuing this testimony beyond my sinful past. Hearing or reading of what is past may give others heart when

L1 *hidden it away]* Psalm 31.1: "Happy those whose evil ways are forgiven, their sins hidden away." Augustine's comment on this psalm explains "hidden away" (literally "covered over") by saying God no longer wants to recognize [*advertere*] them.

L3 *belief and baptism]* In T 8 Augustine himself was strengthened in his progress toward baptism by the stories of other converts (Marius Victorinus, T 8.3–5, and the courtiers of Trier, T 8.15), or Christians' endeavors (Antony, 8.29). Accounts of others' spiritual states were a recognized part of Christian edification, much as addicts' tales of their recoveries are now a part of twelve-step programs.

L6 *strengthens the frail]* 2 Corinthians 12.9: "strength is built up in frailty."

L14 *many have asked]* For the exchange of personal information vouched for by love, see Letter 24.1 in the collection of Augustine's correspondence (*comm.*).

they see how you have forgiven that past, 'have hidden it away,' so I may find happiness in you, after your transformation of my soul by belief and baptism into you. From a slumbrous despair that says it can do nothing, they may wake again to a love of your pity, to the sweetness of your favor, which 'strengthens the frail' by first revealing to them their frailty. The virtuous are interested in the tale of sinners who have repented, not because the sins interest them but because, though they once occurred, they do so no longer.

But what is my motive in testifying not only to my past but to my present condition, writing here for others to read what I am aware of, day by day, as I rely not on any innocence of mine but on expectation of your pity? I have recognized and recorded what use was testimony to my past. Yet many have asked about my condition at this moment of my testifying—both those who know me and those who do not know me personally, but have read something written by me or of me. Though they cannot listen at my heart, which alone could tell them what I really am, still they would like to hear what testimony I can bear to my present interior state, which their own eye or ear or mind cannot reach. Why should they believe my report of what they cannot know directly?—because the love of virtuous people tells them I do not deceive them in my testimony. Their love goes warrant for my credibility.

5.   But what is *their* motive? Would they share my joy when they hear how close, by your gift, I am lifted up to you, and share my prayer when they hear how far, by my own dead

L2 *many give thanks . . . many to pray]*   2 Corinthians 1.11: "You come to our assistance in prayer, so that many shall give thanks for the gift secured by the prayers of many."

L6 *a race of strangers]*   Psalm 143.7–8: "Rescue me from deep waters and from the hand of a race of strangers, the speech of whose mouth is void of meaning, the work of whose strong [right] hand is baneful."

L10 *relief . . . grief]*   The rhyme to approximate the wordplay of *respirent . . . suspirent.*

L15 *an incense]*   Revelation 8.3–4: "Another angel came and stood before the altar holding a golden thurible with much incense in it for censing the golden altar before God's throne with the prayers of all the saints, and the smoke of the incense rose from the angel's hand with the prayers of the saints before God."

L17 *show . . . pity]*   Psalm 50.3: "Show pity to me commensurate with your great pity."

L19 *what you have begun]*   Philippians 1.6: "he who begins his good work in you will complete it in the day of Christ Jesus."

L23 *fearful joy . . . sorrow]*   Psalm 2.11: "Serve the Lord in fear and rejoice with trembling."

L27 *presently accompany]*   For the text (*vitae,* not *viae*), see O 3.164.

weight, I fall off from you? If so, to such I will open myself. For it is not a trivial help, God my Lord, to have 'many give thanks for me or for many to pray for me.' I hope that a brother in spirit will love in me what you show him is lovable, lament in me what you show is lamentable—a brother, not a stranger, not 'a race of strangers, the speech of whose mouth is void of meaning, the work of whose strong hand is baneful,' but one who feels joy at what he approves in me, sorrow at what he disapproves, but feels love in both his joy and his sorrow. To such I will open myself, to those who feel relief for the good, grief for the bad, to be found in me. Since any good lodged in me comes from you, is your boon, while any bad discovered in me is mine, and comes under your ban, their relief will be for the former, their grief for the latter, and their relief's singing or their grief's wailing will rise up to your presence, 'an incense from their heart's thurible, to please you, Lord, with this odor of holiness filling your temple,' so you will 'show pity to me commensurate with your great pity,' with your own honor, and you will 'not abandon what you have begun in me until it is completed.'

6. This, then, is what I hope for in testifying not only to my former but to my present condition—giving testimony, that is, not only in private, with my own 'fearful joy and hopeful sorrow,' but giving it within the hearing of Christian people, companions of my joy as they are sharers of my mortality, members of the same city, on our pilgrim's way to it, all of them who have gone before, or will follow, or presently

L4 *confining/words* . . . *confirming/deeds*] For the play on *loquendo/praeciperet . . . faciendo/praeiret*.

L6 *protecting wings*] Psalm 16.8: "Protect me in the shadow of your wings."

L13 *judge in my own case*] 1 Corinthians 4.3: "I do not judge my own case."

L16 *a man's own spirit*] 1 Corinthians 2.11: "Who can know what is within but a man's own spirit, which is within?"

L20 *I am contemptuous*] Job 42.6: "I am contemptuous of myself, I have faded away, I count myself mere earth and ashes."

L22 *as in a bronze reflection*] 1 Corinthians 13.12: "Now we see cloudily, by a bronze reflection, but then facing you directly." The ancient mirror (*speculum*) was not the bright glass we know, but the comparative murk of polished bronze. "Cloudily"—in obscure form (*in anigmate*).

L23 *my exile*] 2 Corinthians 5.6: "We, while in the body, are in exile from the Lord."

L26 *true to your word*] 1 Corinthians 10.13: "God is true to his word, who will not let you undergo a trial beyond your strength, but he will provide an escape from every trial, to let you survive it."

accompany me. These are your servants and my brothers, your sons whom you make my masters, for me to serve them if I would live with you and because of you. Yet your call to this duty would have little effect if you were just confining it to words and not confirming it by your deeds. To respond to it with my word and my deed I must be 'under your protecting wings,' all helpless before peril were my soul not nestled under those wings, my frailty not allowed for by you. I am nothing in myself, but you my father are at hand, taking special care of me—the one who created me and nurtured me. You, all-powerful, are my all, at one with me before I can be at one with you. To such men, then, as you have ordered me to serve I open myself, not as 'a judge in my own case' but only to be given a hearing by them.

7.   You alone can be my judge. Though 'no one can know what is within but a man's own spirit, which is also within,' there are some inner depths not even the man's own spirit can know, while you, who made those depths, know them through and through. Yet I know certain things about you that I know not about me—though under your scrutiny, 'I am contemptuous of myself, accounting me mere earth and ashes.' Admittedly 'we see now only cloudily, as in a bronze reflection, not as facing you directly,' and in 'my exile' I am farther off from you than from me, yet I know that you can never be overcome, and do *not* know whether this test or that one will overcome me—though I have hope [not knowledge], since 'you are true to your word, and will not let us undergo a trial beyond our

strength, but will provide an escape from every trial, to let us survive it.' Both what I know about myself and what I do not know will therefore be my testimony to you, since what I know I have seen by your light, and what I do not know is from my own darknesses, not yet scattered by your noonday gaze.

L2 *struck a blow]* Augustine thought (*The Teacher* 12) that the word *verbum* came from *verberari* (to be struck so as to resound). The verbum reverberates.

L5 *be any excuse]* Romans 1.20: "From the time when he created the world, God's invisible things are shown to the mind—his everlasting power and godhead—through the things he has made, lest any have excuse [for not recognizing them]."

L6 *have mercy]* Romans 9.14: "I will pity the one I mean to pity, and be merciful to the one I mean to be merciful to."

L8 *what, in loving you]* This book's first of many uses of what O'Donnell calls "the sequence of senses." The sequence is run through four times in **[8]** (*comm.*).

L10 *kindly its aptness to the eye]* Augustine saw sight as active, not simply receiving images on the retina, but emitting the eyes' own rays, which need the cognate rays of the sun to operate—as God's inner light is needed for the mind to operate.

L11 *sweet linkages]* In *The Teacher* 1 Augustine says that "the enjoyment of song comes from the windings of the tune."

L21 *I interrogated]* Another sequence is here, the four elements (*comm.*).

L22 *gave the same testimony]* *Confessa sunt,* one of the many passages that show the real force of *confessio.*

II. The Current Search for God

8. My awareness that I love you is now firm, not wavering—your word struck a blow to my heart, and I love. The very sky and earth, after all, bid me love you, as do all the things (all around me) they contain. They bid every one of us to love, 'lest there be any excuse' for those not loving you (and even then, at a deeper level, 'you will have mercy where your mercy wills, show pity where your pity wills'—why else do heaven and earth reiterate their call to those not hearing them?). But what, in loving you, do I find lovable? Not, surely, physical splendor, nor time's orderliness—not light's clarity (how kindly its aptness to the eye), nor sweet linkages of variable melody; not soft fragrances of flower, oil, or spice; not honey or heaven-bread; not limbs that intermingle in embrace—these are not what, in loving you, I love. And yet I do—*do* love a kind of light, a kind of song or fragrance, food or embrace—in loving you, who are my light and voice and fragrance and food and embrace, all of them deep within me, where is my soul's light that fades not, its song that ends not, a fragrance not dispersed in air, a taste never blunted with satiety, an embrace not ending in depletion. This is what, in loving my God, I love—yet what can I call this?

9. I interrogated the earth, which replied, I am not it—and all earth's contents gave the same testimony. 'I interrogated

L1 *the sea, its depths]* Job 28.14: "The Abyss said, 'It is not in me,' and the Sea said, 'It is not with me.' "

L4 *Anaximenes]* The ancient Ionic philosopher who thought moist air the basic material of the universe.

L10 *their response]* The splendors of God's creation not only speak to the soul. They "testify": *Pulchritudo eorum confessio eorum,* "Their beauty is their testimony" (*Sermon* 241.2)—another passage giving us the range of *confessio*'s meanings.

L22 *The inward humanity]* Romans 7.22: "I take joy in God's law, by my inward humanity."

the sea, its depths' with their slithery inhabitants, which informed me: We are not your God, go higher. I interrogated the veering winds, and the entire atmosphere, with its winged breed, replied to me: Anaximenes was wrong, I am no God. I interrogated the cosmos—sun, moon, stars—which said: No more are we that God you are in quest of. So I addressed the entirety of things thronging at the portals of my senses: Tell me then of the God you aren't, tell me *something* at least. And, clamorous together, they came back: He is what made us. My interrogation was nothing but my yearning, and their response was nothing but their beauty.

At that point, I steered me toward myself, asking me: Who then are you? And I answered myself: A man. Which brought to my mind two things belonging to me, body and soul, one external to me, one internal. Through which of these two should I search for God? I had already used my body to inquire after God from earth and sky, so far as my sight could venture out toward him. Better now to use the interior. It was this self, after all, to which all the body's messages had been reported back, for it to take charge of and evaluate the responses made by heaven and earth and all their denizens, reporting: We are not God, he made us. 'The inward humanity' gained intelligence from its exterior subalterns, but it was I within, the self, the mind acting through my body's sense, who directed the interrogation of the sun's physical stuff, and it was to me that it answered: I am not he, he made me.

10. Is not their beauty evident to all who can perceive it with their senses? Then why does it not deliver to all the same

L2 *adjudicating rationality*] *Judex ratio*: The image is of Augustine's mind setting up court to judge the testimony being reported to it from the creatures his senses interrogated.

L4 *God's invisible things*] Romans 1.20: "God's invisible things are shown to the mind through the things he has made."

L16 *How so?*] Reading *viden* (short for *videsne*, "do you see").

L18 *activate the body's bulk*] *Tu vegatas molem corporis*—cf. Virgil, *Aeneid* 6.727: *mens agitat molem*, "brain activates the bulk."

L26 *a horse, a mule*] Psalm 31.9: "Do not be like the horse or mule, which lack intellect."

message? I do not mean to beasts, of course, large or little, since they can see but not interrogate the beauty—they have no adjudicating rationality, to assess what their senses report to them. Men, however, can by interrogation 'see God's invisible things through the things he has made'—unless attachment to the visible enslaves them, disqualifying them, as slaves, from sitting in judgment. For the visible things do not answer interrogation divorced from judgment—not because the physical creation changes its summons (that is, its beauty) according to whether a man merely sees it, or sees it and interrogates it, but because one and the same beauty is silent to the one while speaking to the other. Or, rather, it speaks to all, but only those hear who bring the outward report before the inner judge of truth—the very truth that tells me: Your God cannot be heaven, or earth, or anything material. Those things say this by their very nature. How so? By their mere bulk, less in its parts than in the whole, a point in which you excel them, my soul—if I may speak to you [instead of them]—since you activate the body's bulk, providing it with life, a service no body can perform for another body (though God animates you, the body's animator).

11.   So what, in loving God, do I love? One who is higher than my own soul's highest point? Then from that part of the soul I must strive up toward him—not through the soul's adhesion to the body, giving life to all its assemblage of parts. Not through that connection will I find God—or then 'a horse, a mule, lacking intellect,' might find God, since they too animate their own bodies. What, then, of another power of the soul over

L1 *conferring . . . confining*]   For the play on *qua vivifico . . . qua sensifico.* Augustine makes up the latter word for this context, to make the soul assign to each sense a sphere more specific than the life bestowed on the whole body.

L5 *single center*]   The mind directs the various senses with a shared sense *(sensus communis).*

the body that God has made for me—a power not only conferring life on the whole body but confining its senses to separate
duties, assigning the eye not to hear, the ear not to see, but each
of the several senses to perform its proper office with its proper
instrument, while the single center of all these diverse actions
is my mind? Even from that I must strive higher, since horses
and mules have this power too, perceiving things by means of
their body.

L2 *pass over . . . striving up]* The verbs *transeo* and *ascendo* are used for the ascent of the mind toward God that resembles the Neoplatonic project, an exercise Augustine repeats at various stages of *The Testimony*.

L4 *lawns and spacious structures]* The "interior landscape" again.

L5 *representations]* For *imagines*, see *terms*.

L6 *further expressions we derive]* *Quidquid etiam cogitamus* (see *terms*).

L16 *memory's gaze]* Literally, "memory's face." Like the "heart's hand" of this passage, an example of the way Augustine thinks of "the inner man" in literal terms. Compare the "mind's mouth" and memory's "stomach" at **[22]**.

L22 *means of accession]* A fifth use of the sequence of senses, in the customary order: sight, sound, smell, taste, touch.

III. The Contents of Memory

1. *Representations* (imagines)

12.   So I must pass over that faculty in my makeup, striving up by degrees toward its maker—which brings me out onto the lawns and spacious structures of memory, where treasure is stored, all the representations conveyed there by any of my senses, along with the further expressions we derive from those representations by expanding, contracting, or otherwise manipulating them; everything ticketed here and stored for preservation (everything that has not been blotted out in the interval, everything not buried in oblivion). Some things, summoned, are instantly delivered up, though others require a longer search, to be drawn from recesses less penetrable. And all the while, jumbled memories flirt out on their own, interrupting the search for what I want, pestering: Wasn't it us you were seeking? My heart's hand strenuously waves these things away from my memory's gaze, until the dim thing sought arrives at last, fresh from depths. Yet other things are brought up easily, in proper sequence from beginning to end, and laid back in the same order, recallable at will—which happens whenever I recite a literary passage by heart.

13.   Here all these things are stored, individually and by type, according to their means of accession—light, for instance,

L3 *whole sensory apparatus*]   Though touch is normally put last in the list of senses, Augustine gives it a more pervasive knowing system than one might expect.

L4 *inner or outer feel of things*]   Augustine mentions things like the sense of weight pressing on the body, which is more than a surface feel of the skin. Similarly, the feel of rough or smooth things in the mouth does not fit easily under the sensation of taste. But the feeling of the sex organ during penetration is the most obvious reason for including this inner aspect of touch. This shows how Augustine's systematic inclusiveness does not shrink from aspects of his life now forgone.

and all colors and physical shapes coming in by way of the eyes; but by the ears all varieties of sound; by the nostril all odors; by the mouth all tastes; and by the body's whole sensory apparatus the inner or outer feel of things, whether they be hard or soft, hot or cold, smooth or rough, heavy or light; all received for deposit in or withdrawal from memory's huge vault—with secret chambers deep beyond scrutiny or description—where each item is filed according to its entry point.

Not that the things come in themselves—sensible representations of them are vividly at hand for expression in the memory. Though it is obvious which sense seized each, and brought it in for storage, who can say how these images are formed—for when I sit in a darkness without sound, I can recall colors at will (singling out black or white or what else I prefer), without any sounds to cut across or jumble the visual image, since sounds, though they are stored in memory, are kept in different compartments. I can bring them up, on call whenever I want, to sing what song I like with my tongue not moving, my throat not sounding, and with no color images that might block or break up the return of some masterpiece from the stock my ears supplied. The variety of things, by my various senses selected and collected, are at my memory's disposal. I can, while smelling nothing, identify the wafture from a lily, contrast it with that from a violet. While tasting or touching nothing, I prefer in memory honey to wine, smooth things to rough.

14.   All these things I transact within me, in memory's immense courtyard, where sky and earth and sea are present to

L2 *I bump up*]   The Latin *mihi et ipse occurro meque* jams together the personal words to enact this odd encounter with a self that is only his by recovery in memory, yet is a kind of "found object" in this catalogue of other things in his memory. This shows how identity can only be established by way of prior alienation from the self (Introduction 3).

L5 *took on trust*]   Things "credited" (*credita*) are all those matters that one does not have direct and personal knowledge of, including the truths of faith that are taken on trust from God.

L6 *new and ever-newer*]   *Alias atque alias*, literally "otherwise and otherwise," to describe altered representations achieved by manipulation of the *imagines*.

L7 *I recombine*]   Literally, "I weave into" (*contexo*). The process of constructing hypothetical future actions is a complex one of first combining images in "new and newer" ways, and then reinserting these into past images to complete a process of rational forecast (Introduction 2).

L12 *this will follow*]   For memory's predictive powers, see Introduction 4.

L15 *store of memory*]   Even the future can be "foreseen" only in memory.

L25 *Then how is it itself?*]   Literally, "Then how not contain [*itself*]?" The point of the argument is in that understood "itself."

L26 *Men go out*]   Petrarch described the role of this sentence in his "mountain epiphany." Having toiled up a high mount, whose massive integrity rebuked him for a divided life, he took out his pocket Augustine and opened, providentially, to this sentence. "I was dumbfounded, I must admit . . . I closed the book, angry at myself that just now I was a gazer at earth's wonders, though I should have learned already, even from pagan sages, that no marvel can compare with the mind, that beside this great thing nothing is great" (Petrarch, *Letters on Informal Topics* 4.1.28). Cf. Cicero, *Republic* 1.30 (quoting Ennius): "No one pays attention to what is at one's feet, all study heavens' distances"; referred to at **[25]**.

L28 *stars' revolvings*]   Wisdom 13.2: "They have taken as gods . . . the stars' revolvings [*gyros*]."

me, and whatever I sensed in them (except those I have forgotten). And this is where I bump up against myself, when I call back what I did, and where, and when, and how I felt when I was doing it. Here are all the things I experienced myself or took on trust from others. From this store of things there are new and ever-newer representations of my experiences, or of things accepted in the past on the basis of trust. These I recombine with representations of the past to ponder future actions, their consequences and possibilities, all considered (once more) as present. Within that vast inner chamber of my mind, stocked with representations of so great number and so great variety, I say to myself: This I shall do, or that—and this will follow, or that will. I say to myself: If only this would happen, or that would! Or: God keep me from this, or from that. And the minute I say it, from that vast treasure store of memory the representations of what I am describing [as in the future] are supplied at once—I could not say any of those things if the representations were not available to me.

15.   Vast, my God, is the power of memory, more than vast in its depths, immense and beyond sounding—who could plumb them to their bottom? Even though this is a power of my own mind, it is what I *am*, still I cannot take it all in. The mind is too limited to contain itself—yet where could the uncontained part of itself be? Outside itself, and not in itself? Then how is it itself? Over and over I wonder at this, dumbfounded by it. Men go out to wonder at mountain heights, at immense sea surges, the sweep of wide rivers, the ocean's range, 'the stars' revolvings'—and neglect [the spectacle of]

L6 *ocean, whose existence]*   Augustine told a friend (Letter 7) that some things not personally experienced (e.g., the taste of a strawberry) cannot be remembered. But the memory can put together synthesized concepts—e.g., the ocean as a vast expanse of water—on the basis of analogous experiences and the word of others.

L13 *liberal studies]*   The seven liberal arts that Augustine studied professionally, and which he planned, after his baptism, to make the basis of a Christian education. The project was broken off by his calling to the priesthood, though he would have abandoned it anyway when he reached a different judgment on its usefulness. But he thought of the arts as disciplines not relying on the senses, which is the point of their inclusion here.

L17 *nature of grammar]*   Augustine gives here the first three subjects (the *trivium*) of liberal studies: grammar, logic, rhetoric. See *comm.*

L20 *some sight outside me]*   He is thinking of a *visual* object of perception, since this begins the sixth use of the sequence of senses.

themselves. They do not even wonder that when I spoke of all these things, my eyes were not seeing them, though I could not have spoken unless my memory was seeing them internally, and on the same huge scale on which they were seen externally—not only the mountains and seas, the rivers and stars which I have seen myself, but also the ocean, whose existence I can take only on trust. I did not engorge the things I saw, the things themselves are not inside me, but their representations are—and I can tell through which sense each one came.

2. *Rules* (percepta)

16. Nor does this exhaust the memory's capacity, since any of the rules I have not forgotten, yet, from my liberal studies are also contained here. They are lodged, as it were, in a space more remote from my exterior (though it cannot really be a space), where I do not possess representations of a thing but the thing itself. The nature of grammar, the art of logical argument, the topics of rhetoric—I know these in such a way that they are immediately present in my memory, not by way of the representation of some sight outside me. That indeed, is how sounds [as well as sight] are represented, since they come and go, like a song that strikes the ear, leaving its pattern for me to remember as if it were still being sung when it is not. An odor, in the same way, drifts by and is dispersed in air, but has so acted on the nostrils that it left in memory its representation—to be, by remembering, re-experienced. Food can no longer be tasted

L9 *topics posed in rhetoric]* For the inclusion of these philosophical problems in *rhetorical* training, see *comm.* **[18]**.

L12 *in my ear]* O'Donnell points out (3.182) that words were primarily *heard* in Augustine's culture, not read. They were entrusted to the ear, not the eye, before literacy became the norm.

L18 *gateways of my body]* A seventh use of the sequence of senses.

when it is being digested, though the memory in some way tastes it still. And anything felt by the body on contact with it can be remembered after that contact is broken. All these things do not themselves go into the memory. Their representations are absorbed—with wondrous celerity, and filed in wondrous receptacles, and wondrously rendered back in the act of remembering.

17. But when, by contrast, I hear that there are three topics posed in rhetoric—whether a thing exists, what is its essence, and what are its accidents—I do indeed keep representations of the words in which these subjects were sounded out, and realize that the words reverberated in my ear during their passage, then faded away. But what was described in those words I never absorbed through my senses, never beheld except in my mind; so my memory retains not any representations of these things, only the things themselves—and let them tell me, if they can, how they came to be inside me. I patrol all the gateways of my body, and find no entry point for these things. My eyes say: Had they been colored shapes, we would have ushered them in. My ears say: If they had made a noise, we would have conveyed it to you. My nostrils say: If they had wafted an odor, we would have passed it along. My taste sense says: Unless they can be savored, make no inquiry of me. Touch says: Unless it had bodily shape, I could not feel it; and if I cannot feel it, I cannot report on it. Whence, then, and through what channel came these subjects into my memory? It stumps me. For when I learned them, I was not taking them

L4 *already in my mind]*   Many take this as a reference to the Platonic notion that all learning is remembering (*anamnesis*) from a previous existence; but see *comm.*

L9 *expressed these truths]*   For *cogitare*, see t*erms.*

L10 *provided an occasion]*   In *The Teacher,* Augustine had argued that others do not really teach us. All they do is "post a sign" (*admonere*) to direct our attention to something we judge on our own. M. F. Burnyeat translates *admonere* in that dialogue as "provide an occasion" (*Proceedings of the Aristotelian Society,* 1987, p. 15).

L10 *brought up from below]*   The verb *eruo* means to unearth, to bring to light. The elements for Augustine's "ex-pressing" his knowledge were there, but he had to be alerted to their presence.

L14 *in and for themselves inside us]*   Emphatic *per se ipsa intus.*

L25 *pressed up . . . pressed . . .* expression]   For the interplay here on *ex-cogitare, cogenda, cogito, cogo,* see *comm.*

on trust from some other person's convictions, but accepting them on my own, establishing their truth, then filing them in my mind where I could withdraw them when I want to. Were they already in my mind—but not in my memory—before I learned them? Where, then? And why, when these matters were simply stated, did I instantly assent, and say: Of course, it must be so? Or were they in memory after all, but stored there deep, behind other things, in secret crevices, so I might not ever have expressed these truths to myself had not someone provided an occasion for their being brought up from below?

18.   We can conclude, then, that to learn these things—those, namely, whose representations are not pulled into us through the senses, but directly perceived, in and for themselves inside us, with no aid at all from the senses—is to express in a connected way what was latent in the memory (but scattered about in disorder), and to make provision for their manageable arrangement (so that the scattered and disordered elements are reduced to a state readily accessed for the mind's use). What a quantity of such items my memory is stocked with, things discovered and (as I said) kept ready for use, the kind of things we say we have learned already and continue to know. Yet if I forgo their retrieval, even for brief intervals, they sink out of sight again, sliding deep into some inner windings, and they must be pressed up out of that place (for where else could they have gone?) and pressed again into knowable form. We must, that is, reconnect them after their dispersion. This is what we mean by *expression*, which comes from pressing, as

L1 exaction...extending]   I supply English parallels to Augustine's Latin examples. He indicates that the *-ito* suffix extends a verb's action in time, when *ago* becomes *agito,* or *facio* becomes *facito.* In a similar way, the English prefix *ex-* extends in space.

L8 *mathematics and geometry]*   Augustine moves on to the sphere of the other four liberal arts, the *quadrivium* of mathematics, geometry, music, and astronomy, which are even more remote from sensible experience than the subjects of the *trivium.* For these and their "extensibility," see *comm.*

L10 *colored, audible...tangible]*   The eighth use in this book of the sequence of senses.

L24 *exist apart]*   The immaterial ideas are valid in their own right (*valde sunt*).

L25 *may mock]*   He is referring to materialists, who cannot conceive mental concepts entirely divorced from physical reality. Since Augustine was for years a materialist himself (T 7.1–2), he is condoling (*doleam*) with his former colleagues rather than returning their mock. Petrarch said that people were still mocking Augustine in the fourteenth century: "Read *The Testimony,* which some laughable people regularly laugh at" (*Letters on Informal Topics* 10.3).

exaction comes from acting, or *extension* comes from tending. In fact, this is a concept so commandeered mentally that *an expression* no longer means anything pressed-out in a general way, but common usage reserves it for what is expressed *in thought*.

3. *Axioms* (rationes)

19. The memory also contains the endlessly extensible rules and axioms of mathematics and geometry, none of which is borne in upon memory through the senses, since none of them is colored, audible, scented, flavored, or tangible. Admittedly, when these sciences were being discussed, I heard words describing their axioms, but the words were not the same thing as the axioms, since the Greek language uses different words from the Latin for what are themselves neither Greek nor Latin concepts, or those of any other language. If I look at an architect's depiction of dimensions, even if they are drawn in lines as tenuous as a spider's thread, these sensible images are not geometric lines, which no sensible images can convey through the eye. These one knows from within, without the need for giving them any physical expression. In the same way I count with the senses of my body the number of external things, but the numbers of mathematics, by which we number, are not the same as numbered things, nor are they the representation of such things. They exist apart from them. One who cannot see such bodiless numbers may mock me for speaking thus, but I condole with him for mocking thus.

L11 *a memory of past remembering]*   This overlay of memories constantly being linked and mutually altered is important to Augustine's view of the way identity is constructed.

L15 *mental reactions]*   For *affectiones,* see *terms.*

L26 *mind remembering itself]*   Memory is the principle of identity, but it is also a principle of disjunction. I am what I remember myself to be, yet the remembered me is not the same as the remembering me (Introduction 3).

20. All these things I not only remember but remember learning them. And many arguments against them I remember hearing; and however false the arguments may be, my memories of hearing them are not false. And I remember distinguishing between what was true and what was said against the truth—an act of distinguishing I remember one way now, which is different from the way I remember often going over the distinction while I was expressing it. I remember these frequent acts from the past, and what I distinguish and conclude now I am laying away in memory, so I can remember in the future what I conclude at this moment. So, just as I have a memory of past remembering, so in the future, if I recall what I conclude now, I shall be recalling it by the power of memory.

4. *Reactions* (affectiones)

21. The mental reactions I experienced are also in my memory, but not with the relation the mind had to those reactions while undergoing them—in a different way, rather, according to the relation memory has with itself. For I can remember being happy, without being happy as I remember; or remember being sad, without being sad; or fearlessly recall being afraid, or sinlessly recall sinful desire. As a matter of fact, remembered sorrows can comfort, remembered joys distress me. There is nothing odd about this if I am remembering bodily sensations, for the mind is not the same thing as the body, and why should it be odd for the body's pain to be remembered to the mind's comfort? But this is a case of the mind remembering itself—why else would we commit something to

L14 *categories of excitement*]   For *perturbationes*, see *terms*. The four that
Augustine names are the standard "excitements." The Stoics aspired to rise
above them to a state of *apatheia* (imperturbability). Augustine saw a proper
role for the excitements (which can excite us to feel joy in God, or to feel sorrow for sin). See *Interpreting John's Gospel* 60.3: "Christians should feel these
excitements for the proper reasons, and not join the Stoics and their like, who
mistake vanity for verity and coma for composure [*vanitatem/veritatem, stu-
porem/sanitatem*]."

L21 *decanted*]   With *depromi*, Augustine imagines old memories brought up
like a wine to be savored, a Horatian topos (*comm.*).

L23 *mind's mouth*]   With this, and with memory's "stomach," compare "the
heart's hand" and "memory's gaze" at [12].

memory by saying: *Be sure to keep this in mind?* Or, when forgetting, say: *That does not come to mind?* Or: *It has slipped my
mind*—equating memory and mind? But if this is so, why is it
that, when I take joy in remembered sorrow, the mind is happy
at the memory's sorrow? How can the mind rejoice because it
contains joy, but the memory not be sad because it contains
sorrow? Is memory separable from mind after all? How could
we claim that? The memory must, instead, be a kind of mental
belly, where happiness and sorrow are like sweet and sour food,
which—once they are digested—are retained but no longer
tasted. The analogy is admittedly undignified, but not without
a partial basis.

22. It will be clear that I am drawing on my memory when I say that the mind has four categories of excitement—desire, joy, fear, and sorrow. And it is in memory that I
find and produce whatever reasonings I can make about them,
distinguishing them by genus and species, and defining each.
Yet I am not excited by these excitements when I recur to them
by remembering them. Before they were identified in memory,
and called up from it, they had to be laid away there, otherwise
I could not have decanted them by the act of memory. Could
they be recalled from memory as food is belched from the
stomach? But why, in that case, does the expressive mind's
mouth not do what the body's does—experience again the
sweetness or the bitterness of recalled joy or sorrow in the act
of renewing the memory? Does the analogy fail because they
are unlike in this respect? If they *were* alike in this way, too,
who would want to discuss sorrow or fear, when every time we

mentioned them we had to be sad or frightened? Yet we could not discuss them at all without having in memory the meaning of those excitements registered formerly by our senses—we do not recall merely the names for them, but the meaning as well. This meaning does not come from outside the mind through any bodily aperture—rather, the mind conceives the meaning while it is undergoing the impact made on the body's senses, and lodges that meaning in memory.

23.   Unless memory performs the act on its own—for who can be certain that the representations of the passions do not themselves cause the memory? When I use the word for, say, a stone, or the sun, even though the things themselves are not present to my senses, their representations are on call in my memory. Similarly, when I use the word for pain, it is not present to my senses if I am not hurting at the moment. Still, I could not know what is meant by the name for pain unless a representation of it were in my memory; nor, in conversation with others, could I distinguish it from pleasure. And even if I pronounce the word for health when I am healthy, thus experiencing the thing itself, I would not be remembering unless the representation of health were in my memory, any more than the sick could recognize what the word health signifies unless what is not in their body were supplied from what is in their memory. But when I pronounce the word for numbers, for what we use in counting things, it is not their representation that is in my memory. Number itself is there. If I refer to a representation of the sun, and I am remembering it, it is not the

L5 *access to itself*]   Memory, as the seat of identity, cannot be a representation of something alien from the self. Yet it seems not as directly presented to itself as sensible experience or the apprehension of number (*comm.*).

L17 *a lack of memory*]   *Privatio memoriae.* Forgetfulness is a real mystery to Augustine, not a mere intellectual ploy here. All privation is mysterious to him. His definition of evil is *defectus entis*, lack of being, as his definition of error is *defectus veritatis*. Since man is not a perfect being like God, he traffics of necessity with non-being, the more so as he departs from God. Forgetting is therefore a sign of man's imperfection; but what puzzles Augustine here is that he can still claim the forgetting as his own, *his* lack, by remembering that he forgot. In the same fashion we "own" the non-being of our sins, and the non-being of our errors.

representation of the representation I recall, but the representation of the thing. That is what I have on call in my memory.
And if I pronounce the name for memory, and recognize what I
am pronouncing, where does that recognition take place but in
the memory? So memory must have an immediate access to
itelf, not intermediated through a representation of itself.

5. *Forgetting* (oblivio)

24.   But if I say the word for forgetting, I recognize what is
referred to, and how would I recognize it if I were not remembering it? It is not merely the sound of the word I recognize,
but what it signifies. Unless I were remembering that, the
sound of the word would have no effect on me, and I could
not effect any understanding to it. So, though memory is in
my memory when I remember remembering, both forgetting and remembering are in my memory when I remember
forgetting—remembering *that* I forget, and forgetting *what*
I once remembered. What can forgetting be but a lack of
memory? And then how can forgetting be present, for me to
remember it, when its very presence makes me lack it? All
things we remember are in our memory—and since we must
remember forgetting, or we would not know what the word
means when we hear it, then forgetting must be in our
memory. It is there for us to remember, but its being there
means we forget. Or should we say that forgetting is not there
itself when we remember it, but only some representation of it,
since its being present itself would make us lack memory? Who
can fathom such a thing, or make any sense of it?

L2 *terrain of trouble]* Genesis 3.17: "Earth will be doomed for you to labor at it."

L2 *sweat of my brow]* Genesis 3.19: "In the sweat of your brow you will have food to eat." The echo is not empty, since forgetfulness is one of the penalties of original sin, like other frailties and mortality itself.

L3 *studying heaven's distances]* Ennius, quoted by Cicero at *Republic* 1.30: "No one pays attention to what is at one's feet, but all study heaven's distances [*plagas*]."

L4 *poising earth on balance]* Job 28.25: "He poised the meted winds on balance."

25.   Here I labor at hard material, Lord, and I *am* that material. I am 'a terrain of trouble,' worked with much 'sweat of my brow.' What we are doing here is not, after all, 'studying heaven's distances,' not measuring interstellar spaces, not 'poising earth on balance.' I am what I am remembering, my own mind. It is no surprise for some non-me to be distant from me, but what is nearer to me than I myself? I cannot understand myself when I am remembering, yet I cannot say anything about myself without remembering myself. And what am I to make of the fact that I am positive that I remember having forgotten? Shall I say that what I remember is not in my memory? Or that forgetting is in my memory, to remind me to forget? Both are the purest nonsense.

Is there a third way to pose the matter? How about claiming that I do not remember forgetting but only the representation of forgetting? Yet how can I say that, when a representation of forgetting could be present in memory only if there had been, in the first place, a forgetting to be represented? That is how I remember Carthage or other places I have been, the faces I have seen, the external things I have been alerted to by my senses, or my body's own health or sickness. When these things were presented to me, memory took representations of them for my present consideration, or for later recollection if I remembered them in their absence. So if I remember not forgetting itself, but forgetting's representation, then forgetting must have been present when the representation was formed from it. Yet if forgetting is made present to the mind, how can its representation be taken into the memory when its very presence

L5 *adaptabilities]* Some (see O 3.187) take *multiplicitas* as parallel to the invocation of "my God." I translate it as adaptabilities to suggest how far from God's unity is the note of variation in *multi-plicitas* (literally, "many-twiningness," from *plecto*).

L23 *my sweet illumination]* Ecclesiastes 11.7: "Sweet is illumination, and a delight for eyes to see the sun."

L25 *embrace you]* Psalm 72.38: "Good it is for me to embrace the Lord."

means the cancellation of what is memorized? Yet wild and inexplicable as all this may be, how can I deny that forgetting, which wipes out memory, is something I do remember?

26.   The scope of memory is vast, my God, in some way scary, with its depths, its endless adaptabilities—yet what are they but my own mind, my self? Then what can that self be, my God? What is my makeup? A divided one, shifting, fierce in scale. In memory alone there are uncountable expanses, hollows, caverns uncountably filled with uncountable things of all types—some of them representations, like those of sensible objects; some present without need for representation, like the tenets of the liberal arts; while others are there by some mysterious registration process, like the mind's reactions, which the memory retains though the mind is no longer experiencing those reactions—still, if in the memory, how not in the mind? I rummage through all these things, darting this way and that, plunging down as far as I can go, and reaching no bottom. Such, then, is memory's force, this lifeforce in the living man who dies.

My God, you who are my real life, what course is left me [reaching no bottom of memory]? I will pass over even this force in me called memory, pass over it while venturing toward you, 'my sweet illumination.' Are you telling me this? Striving up through my own faculties to you who are above them, in an effort to reach you where you are reachable, to 'embrace you where embraceable,' I will pass beyond the scope of what is called my memory—for even birds and beasts have memory (or how could they find again their nests or dens, or whatever

L3 *sundered me]* Job 35.11: "He sunders me from quadrupeds, makes me wiser than the flighty birds."

L8 *the woman ... lamp]* Luke 15.8: "A woman who owns ten drachmas and loses one—will she not light her lamp, scour the house, and keep doggedly searching until it is found?"

other places they haunt, which could only become their haunts because remembered by them?). So I will pass beyond my memory in quest of him 'who sundered me from quadrupeds and made me wiser than the flighty birds.' I will pass beyond memory to find you—where? Where, my sure and loving stay, shall I find you? If I find you beyond memory, is that not to forget you—would I be finding by forgetting you?

27.   The woman [of the gospel], who lost her coin and went looking for it with a lamp, could not have found it unless she remembered what she was looking for. Even if found, how could it be recognized as the one she lost if she no longer remembers what she lost? I remember having lost many things myself, which I found again; and while I was looking, if anyone asked me whether this or that was it, I kept answering no until what I was looking for turned up. If I had not remembered what was lost, I would not have recognized it when it turned up. That is always the case when one searches for lost things and finds them. If we happen to lose sight of a thing, but not the memory of it, its representation is preserved within, and it is searched for till restored to sight. Then it is recognized by matching it with its internal representation. We could not say we had found what was lost if we did not recognize it, and we could not recognize it without the memory of it, since it was lost to sight but not to memory.

28.   But what if the memory should itself lose something— as happens when we forget something and try to remember it? Where should we go looking for it but in the memory [that lost it]? And if something else than what we look for turns up, we

L11 *click*] Literally, "fit together" (*conectitur*).

L14 *affords us the occasion*] Another word (*commoneo*) to show that no one ever really teaches us.

L25 *life for my soul I look for*] Psalm 68.33: "Look for the Lord and your soul will have life."

reject it until the right thing comes along—upon which we say: Here it is. That is a thing we could not say without recognizing it, nor recognize without remembering it—despite the fact that we *had* forgotten it. Or had all of it not slipped the mind, but a part of it remained to make us seek what was lost, as if the memory had some feeling that it was not moving with something it had moved with before, but was limping, as it were, from the lack of what it was used to, and trying to recover what was missing. If, for instance, we see or express in the mind someone we know, but try in vain to remember his name, any other name that comes to mind does not click. Since it did not express the man in the past, it is rejected—unless, of course, the right one comes to mind, and its exact fit is acknowledged. What could establish that but memory? Even if another affords us the occasion to remember [by supplying the name], that occasion is provided for the memory's activity. We would not accept it on trust, as if new to us, but acknowledge only what tallies with our memory. If the name had been entirely expunged from memory, we would not remember it even when given the occasion to—so even things we remember we forget are not entirely forgotten. If they were, we could not still be looking for them.

6. *Happiness* (beata vita)

29.   But how, Lord, do I look for you? In looking for you, I seek the happy life. It is 'life for my soul I look for,' since you vivify the soul as the soul vivifies the body. How shall I look for this life of happiness? I do not yet have it, or I could say: This is

L13 *withheld or held]* To approximate the play on *spe beati* and *re beati* in the text.

L20 *all together]* Augustine sets aside for now a theory that obviously attracts him—that human solidarity in Adam gives us some primordial memory of Eden as well as of the sin that forfeited it. This would differ from individual pre-existence of the Platonic sort. See John M. Rist, *Augustine: Ancient Thought Baptized* (New York: Cambridge University Press, 1994), pp.121–34.

L21 *in whom we all have died]* 1 Corinthians 15.22: "As in Adam all die, so in Christ shall all be given life."

all I need. Whereas now I can only say that I am still looking for it—do I have some memory of it, at least as a thing forgotten but which I remember having forgotten? Or is it an unknown thing some instinct for knowledge prompts me to discover—a thing unknown entirely, or unknown in the sense that I no longer remember having forgotten it? What is a life of happiness but what all men want, what none can *not* want? Where caught they some report of what they should want, where some glimpse of what they should love? Somehow, I know not how, we do want it. People may at times experience a certain degree of happiness, or a sense of withheld happiness. This is not the held happiness of those in heaven, yet it is better than having no happiness, either withheld or held. And some kind of happiness even the unhappy have, enough to know what they want (as indeed they do continue wanting).

Somehow or other they have caught a glimpse of happiness, provided them by some or other way of knowing, which puzzles me—was it by remembering happiness? If so, we must have known some prior happiness. It is not my present inquiry whether we knew it separately, or all together in the man who committed original sin, 'in whom we all have died,' and from whom we are all descended in sorrow. No, I ask simply if happiness is a thing remembered—for how could we love it if we could not recognize it? As soon as we hear the word for happiness, we admit that is what we all crave. It is not the word that draws us—when a person speaking Greek hears the name for it in Latin, he is not drawn to it, not recognizing what is meant; but we who speak Latin are drawn by it, as the Greek speaker

L27 *eyes or ears . . . fingers]*   The ninth use of the sequence of five senses.

would be to his own word for the same thing; since joy itself is not Greek or Latin, but the thing all Greeks and Romans pant to acquire, as do the speakers of every other language. All have the concept of happiness, and all would answer yes if asked whether they want it—which could not happen if happiness, and not merely the word for it, were not remembered.

30. But is it remembered as one remembers having seen Carthage? Hardly. For happiness is not seen by the eye, like a physical object. Do we remember happiness, then, as we remember mathematical truths? Not that either, for those who know those truths are not still trying to acquire them, while we who know enough about happiness to love it, are still trying to acquire it, to *be* happy. Well, then, is this like remembering persuasiveness? Not really. Some who understand the word when they hear it are not themselves persuasive; and many would like to be persuasive, which shows they have some understanding of what it is—but they have observed with their senses the persuasiveness of other people, which pleased them and made them want to acquire it, a pleasure that shows some inner grasp of its meaning, and a desire to acquire based on that pleasure, while we have not grasped the meaning of happiness from observing others with our physical senses.

Can it be that we have an idea of happiness from memories of our own joyful experiences? Perhaps. For I can, though sorrowing, remember joy, looking back on the happy life in a state of desolation, and the joy was not being experienced by my eyes or ears or nostrils or tongue or fingers. Rather, it was something the mind experienced during a past period of happiness,

L9   *remembering it, I should love it]*   The text has simply "I should remember and love and long for it." But O 3.193 points out that these three presents refer to past, present, and future—and are therefore the "three presents" of time in T 11. The interaction of the three in a time-continuum is compendiously suggested.

L13   *determined . . . determined]*   *Certa . . . certa* applied to different but matching entities.

some record of which was lodged in memory, enabling me to recall it, sometimes with revulsion, sometimes with longing, according to the different sources of my memories. Shameful things that once filled me with joy I now remember with disgust and reviling. At other times, joy in virtuous and upright things I recall with longing, if they are gone, and my former joys sadden me.

31.   But happiness [not mere joy]—where or when did I experience that, so that remembering it, I should love it; and loving it I should long for it? And not I alone want this, or some elite I belong to, but everyone without exception wants it. We could not want it with so determined a will had we no equally determined knowledge of it. But how is this knowledge determined? Offer two men a choice—between, say, becoming a soldier or not—and one person will take that course, another refuse it, though both instantly say yes if asked if they hope to be happy. In fact, the one who becomes a soldier hopes that will make him happy, and the man refusing hopes the same. Is this just a matter of individual preference? Even so, they are at one in wanting happiness, just as they would agree in saying that they want delight, which they equate with the happy life. Though they pursue it in different courses of life, yet they are striving toward the same object, that which delights them. And no one can deny he has experienced happiness, since something fixed in his memory responds when the word for it is pronounced.

L3 *joy not given sinners*]   Isaiah 48.22: "There is no joy given sinners, says the Lord."

L12 *flesh's urges*]   Galatians 5.17: "Flesh's urges oppose the spirit, the spirit's oppose the flesh." For *concupiscentia* as "urge," see *terms*.

L19 *my enlightenment*]   Psalm 26.1: "The Lord, my enlightenment and rescue, whom I shall hold in awe."

L20 *the rescue of my honor*]   Psalm 41.7: "the rescue of my honor." Literally, the rescue of my face, but the ability to bear one's face unashamed before others is a symbol of honor.

32. Let me not, Lord, in this my heartfelt testimony to you, accept as happiness every joy that I encounter. There is a 'joy not given sinners,' one given those who freely seek you, who find you are their joy. This is true happiness in life, to take joy in you, for you, because of you—this, nothing else, is happiness. Those who do not know this pursue their joy elsewhere, and though it is no true one, yet they cannot wrench their desire entirely free from some representation of that joy.

33. Or do all men not want happiness after all, since those unwilling to find joy in you, who alone are true happiness, must to that extent *not* be wanting it? Or do all want happiness, but because 'flesh's urges oppose the spirit, and the spirit's oppose the flesh,' they cannot accomplish what they desire, and they settle for what they can accomplish? Incapable of what they desire, they do not desire enough to become capable of it. Yet when I ask anyone if he prefers to find true joy or false, he is as quick to say he wants the true one as he is to say he wants happiness—yet happiness is itself a joy in the truth, and that is a joy in you, God, who are the truth, 'my enlightenment, the rescue of my honor, my God.' You are the happiness that everyone desires, the only happiness. All desire to take joy in the truth. I have met many who enjoy lying to others, but none who enjoy being lied to themselves. How did they learn that there is a happy life but in the way they learned that there is truth? They prove they have a love of truth by not wanting to be lied to—when they show a love for the happy life, which is nothing but a joy in truth, they show to that extent that they love truth as well, and they could not do that if they did not

L5 *light they have]* John 12.35–36: "You have as yet attenuated light, so travel on while your light lasts, that darkness may not overtake you, for one walking in the dark goes he knows not where. So while your light lasts, give it your trust, in order to become sons of light."

L7 *truth itself breed]* Terence, *The Girl From Andros* 68: "Flattery breeds friends, as truth breeds enemies."

L7 *become their foe]* Galatians 4.16: "Do I make myself your foe by telling you the truth?"

L14 *rebuking truth]* John 3.20: "All who do evil hate the light, and shun the light lest their deeds be rebuked by it."

have some sense of it in memory. Then why does not truth it-self give them joy? For the same reason that they are not happy? The memory of true happiness is dimmed by their engagement with things making for unhappiness. 'As yet the light they have is attenuated—let them travel on, keep travel-ing lest darkness overtake them.'

34.   How can 'truth itself breed enmity,' or 'a man become their foe by preaching the truth,' when happiness is what is de-sired, and happiness is joy in truth? Is it because, though truth is loved, other things are also loved, and those loves pass for love of truth? Since they do not want to be deceived, they per-sist in thinking their falsehoods are not deceits. By staying true to what they love they become enemies to the true. They love a supporting but not 'a rebuking truth.' Because they hate to be lied to, but like to lie, they love to find things with the help of truth, but hate to be found out by it. But this is the revenge truth takes on those men unwilling to be found out by it: It not only finds out the truth about them but prevents them from finding it out. To this, even this, is the human mind reduced, to this blind, weak state, that it wants to hide its foul vileness from others, but wants nothing hidden from it. But truth turns this upside down—so that the mind does not hide the truth, but the truth is hidden from it. Yet even so, the miserable thing would still prefer truth to falsehood, and it could be happy if it did not place obstacles in its own way, but rejoiced instead in that truth that makes all things true.

L10 *take delight in]* Psalm 36.4: "Take delight in the Lord, and he will grant what your heart asks for."

L24 *happy, sad . . . fearful]* The four excitements listed again, with remembering and forgetting added to them.

7. *God* (Deus)

35.   See what a long ramble I have made through my own memory in quest of you, Lord, and I have not found you anywhere but inside it. Nothing about you have I found but what I remember from the time I began learning about you. Nor have I forgotten what I early learned of you, for in each truth I learned I was learning about my God, who is truth itself, nor did I forget that. In my memory, then, you have been lodged from the time I first learned of you, and there I find you when I remember you and 'take delight in you,' take the holy delights your pity grants me as you consider my deprivation.

36.   But where in memory can you be lodged, Lord, where lodge you there? What hallowed place have you made for yourself in me? You honor me with your presence as a lodger in my memory, but where you may be lodging I am still to know. While calling you to mind, I went beyond the precincts of memory that even animals manifest, where I did not find you among the representations of physical objects. I moved on, to the precincts where I store my mental reactions, and did not find you there. I entered my mind's chamber, for it too is seated in memory (how else could the mind remember itself?). But you were not there, either. Just as you are not a representation of objects, or the reaction of the soul (whether we are happy, sad, desirous, fearful, remembering, forgetful, or whatever), neither are you the mind, for you are the mind's lord, God, though you deigned to lodge in me from the time of my early memories of you. Why, in fact, am I inquiring where in

L21 *calling to me]* The tenth use of the sequence of the senses, returning to the idea of spiritual senses with which he began **[8]**, rounding off the whole section on memory in one of the most beautiful paragraphs Augustine ever wrote.

L24 *satiation] Pax*. For this and similar words (*quies*) describing the fulfillment of sexual *voluptas* (openly stated as *satietas* in the spritual sequence of senses at **[8]**), see *Truth in Religion* 2.1.

memory you lodge, as if there were physical precincts there? All I can know is that you must be there, since I do have a memory of you from my early days, and there is where I find you when remembering.

37. But where did I find you that I learned about you? You could not have been already in my memory, before that first learning of you. Where could I have found you, for learning about you, but outside of me, and within you? And that could not have been in a place, a place I might enter or leave— surely, there is no such place—for as truth you hold audience anywhere and with anyone who approaches, responding at once to all their different concerns. Clear is your counsel, not always clearly accepted. Your best suppliant is not the one who asks to hear what he wants but to want what he hears.

38. Slow was I, Lord, too slow in loving you. To you, earliest and latest beauty, I was slow in love. You were waiting within me while I went outside me, looking for you there, mis-shaping myself as I flung myself upon the shapely things you made. You were with me all the while I was not with you, kept from you by things that could not be except by being in you. You were calling to me, shouting, drumming on deaf ears. You thundered and lightninged, piercing my blindness. You shed a perfume—inhaling it, I pant for you. For your taste, I hunger and thirst. At your caress, I am feverish for satiation.

L1 *all of me clings]* Psalm 62.9: "My soul has adhered to you."

L2 *sorrow or toil]* Psalm 89.10: "greater than they [our years] is the toil and sorrow."

L10 *man's life on earth]* Job 7.1: "What is man's life on earth but a testing?"

IV. The Flesh's Urges

39. When 'all of me clings to you,' there will be no more 'sorrow or toil' for me, but you will bring my life to life, filling it with you. For I am not yet filled with you, since you draw up what you fill while I weigh myself down with delights I should regret and regrets that should delight me, confused about which will prevail. Pity, oh, take pity on me, as sorrow for past wrong contends with happiness over present good, and which will prevail confuses me. Pity, O Lord, oh take pity on me—you see I am exposing my wounds, the patient before the doctor. Pity the pitiable me. 'What is man's life on earth but a testing'—and who would have chosen its burdens and hindrances? You tell us to bear but not to love them. No one who merely bears a thing is loving it, even if he loves the bearing of it. He may be glad that he can bear it, while preferring that he did not have to. So in affliction I want ease, but when eased I fear affliction. Is there anywhere between the two states, where life might no longer be a testing? Not, surely, in worldly ease, which is twice dangerous, from fear of its reversal or from disintegration by its indulgence. Nor, even more surely, in worldly trial, which is twice and thrice dangerous, making us hope for ease, undergo its own harshness, and lose heart to bear it. Without any remission, therefore, is 'man's life on this earth a testing.'

L2 *Granting whatever . . . will*]   This sentence caused the earliest and bitterest dispute arising from *The Testimony*, since Pelagius attacked it heatedly (*comm.*).

L4 *Since I realized*]   Wisdom 8.21: "Since I realized that no one can be self-disciplined unless God grants it, and knowing who grants it is a mark of wisdom, I went to the Lord and beseeched him."

L12 *the flesh's urges . . . designs*]   1 John 2.16: "For the things of this world—the flesh's urges, the eyes' urges, and worldly designs—are not from the Father." This Johannine text structures the following self-examination under the headings of these three urges. (For *concupiscentiae*, see *terms* and *comm.*).

L12 *the eyes' urges*]   For the special sense here, see *comm.* [55].

L12 *worldly designs*]   *Ambitio saeculi*, where *ambitio* is "maneuvering" (see *comm.*).

L22 *yield to the imagined*]   The issue of freedom from seminal emissions at night was raised by fourth-century ascetics. It had to do not with sin but with a special dispensation for ascetics (*comm.*).

40. I have no hope at all, then, but in your pity for me. Granting whatever you require, require whatever you will. You impose on us self-discipline. Well, as the writer has it, 'Since I realized that no one can be self-disciplined unless God grants it, knowing who grants it is a mark of wisdom.' Self-discipline is a gathering inward, toward oneness, from our dispersal out into severalness. For no one loves you well who loves anything else except because of you. You, my love, who burn forever without consuming, set me on fire, for the charity of God. You impose self-discipline? Require anything, granting what you require. 41. You unmistakably demand that I check 'the flesh's urges, the eyes' urges [to know], and worldly designs.'

1. The Five Senses: Touch

You ordered me to give up my sexual partner—and even marriage, though allowed me, you advised me to forgo. I complied, since you granted me the power, even before I became a priest of your mysteries. Yet there are representations of things formed by preceding habit, and they linger in the very memory I have been delineating—representations that throng on me, though weakly, while I am awake, but with enjoyment in my dreams, where I yield to the imagined act. So strong in my flesh is this fictive representation that sleeping falsehood prevails where waking truth could not. Am I not my real self then, Lord? Is there some border between two different selves which I cross and re-cross in sleeping or waking? What happens in this process to the self-rule that stays strong against such

L1 *unbending under buffetings]* *Inconcussus manet.* In the *Aeneid* (4.444–49), the hero is like an oak whose trunk is buffeted *(concusso)*, but his determination is unbending *(manet).*

L10 *remove with your healing hand]* Psalm 102.3: "he who heals all your symptoms." For *languor* as symptom, see *terms.*

L12 *overflow of bounty]* *Abundantiore gratia,* 1 Timothy 1.14: "The bounty of the Lord has overflowed [*superabundavit gratia*] in faith and the love of Jesus Christ."

L18 *with overflowing bounty]* Ephesians 3.20: "He is able with overflowing bounty to grant more than we ask or could think of asking."

L25 *Cautiously joyful]* Psalm 2.11: "Be cautiously joyful."

promptings, 'unbending under buffetings,' even in the presence of real women? Does it go to sleep because the body's external senses do? In that case, how could we stay strong at
times even in sleep, remembering wakeful resolves to stay
chaste, not yielding to these sensual solicitings? Yet the border
between the two selves remains clear enough that, when we do
fail in dreams, we can awake to a clear conscience. Because of
the distinction between the two states, we did not do willingly
what we regret was done passively in us.

42. Clearly you could, if you would, 'remove with your
healing hand the symptoms of sin' in my soul, to blot out in 'an
overflow of bounty, all lustful stirrings, even in my sleep.
Gradually, by degrees, you will give me strength, that my soul,
still mired in lust, will detach itself and obey myself as I obey
you. Then it will put down its own rebellions against itself, not
greeting the sensual representations with shameful action of
uncleanness, even to seminal emission, but will not want such a
thing, even in sleep. It would not be hard for you, 'able with
overflowing bounty to grant more than we ask or could think
of asking,' to free me, not merely at some stage of my life but at
this one, from finding pleasure in these things, or from finding
more than it would be easy for one chastely disposed to resist,
even in his sleep. Meanwhile I have testified to you, God, who
favor me, that that is not my condition so far with regard
to this flaw. 'Cautiously joyful' for what you have granted,
mournful for what I still lack, I look forward to the completion
of your pitying acts in a final peace, one that will fill my inner

L1 *death is by victory*]   1 Corinthians 15.54: "Then what is written will be fulfilled, that death is by victory obliterated."

L3 *Taste*]   Augustine inverts the ordinary sequence of the senses, delaying till the final (climactic) position the sense of sight, since that is the most serious of his own remaining tests. The eleventh use of the sequence of senses.

L4 *trouble of the day*]   Matthew 6.34: "Each day's trouble is fitted to it."

L7 *blot out both*]   1 Corinthians 6.13: "Food serves the stomach, the stomach food, but God will blot out the one and the other."

L8 *clothing disintegration*]   1 Corinthians 15.53: "Disintegration must be clothed with integrity, and the mortal with immortality."

L11 *treating my body*]   1 Corinthians 9.27: "I punish my body, making it my slave."

L27 *needing … exceeding*]   For the play on *petat* and *suppetat*.

as well as outer self, at the time when 'death is by victory obliterated.'

2. The Five Senses: Taste

43. Another 'trouble of the day' I have, and would it were 'fitted to each one.' For daily our body deteriorates, and we build it back up by eating and drinking—till the time when you 'blot out both food and the stomach,' canceling hunger with a wondrous plenitude and 'clothing disintegration with integrity eternal.' But at present hunger is a sweet compulsion, which I must wrestle into control, lest it overcome me. I treat it as a foe by fasting, 'treating my body as my slave,' yet hunger's pain is only stayed with pleasure—for hunger and thirst are a kind of pain, they burn us like a fever till they be medicined by eating, so we call this crisis of our body a delight, since your soothing gifts, the products of earth and water and sky, accommodate our weakness.

44. As medicine, then, you teach me to use food. But while I pass from hunger's exigence to a soothing plenitude, that very passage takes me into a snare of urges, since the process is so pleasing, and there is no other way of passing from need but what the need itself demands. We eat and drink to maintain our health; but a seductive satisfaction tags along with the act, and sometimes tries to slip ahead of it, so that the pleasure I claim or wish to be using for my health I am actually using for its own sake. It is hard to find the proper match between them, since what is enough for health is too little for pleasure, and it is often hard to distinguish my health needing

L8 *Clog not your hearts]* Luke 21.34: "Take care that your hearts be not clogged with dissolute and drunken ways."

L12 *No one gains]* Wisdom 8.21: "Since I realized that no one can be self-disciplined unless God grants it, and knowing who grants it is a mark of wisdom, I went to the Lord and beseeched him."

L14 *by your gift]* Wisdom 8.21 (see previous note).

L20 *Follow not]* Ecclesiasticus 18.30: "Follow not your urges, but shun indulgence."

L22 *What we eat]* 1 Corinthians 8.8: "Diet does not ingratiate us with God, nor does what we refrain from make us deficient, nor what we eat make us better off." Paul is abjuring the kosher rules for Jewish Christians.

L25 *I have learned]* Philippians 4.11–13: "I have learned to cope with what comes; familiar with being down and out, familiar with good prospects; initiated into all changes of fortune, whether repletion or hunger, plenty or privation; able to do all things in him who strengthens me."

nourishment from my gluttony exceeding indulgence. My soul in its weakness takes advantage of this ambiguity, making a cover of it, happy not to know what health truly demands, making health a mere excuse for stealthy dealings with delight. Try as I may to resist such daily troubles, I call on your intervening arm and turn over the problem to you, since I have not been able to settle it myself.

45. I acknowledge what you have decreed, 'Clog not your hearts with dissolute or drunken ways.' Alcoholism is not my problem (may your pity keep me far from it), but gluttony subtly steals over me, even in your service. May your pity also keep me far from that, as 'No one gains self-discipline but by your grant.' What we ask in prayer you often bestow—but a thing bestowed before we ask is equally your gift. And 'by your gift' we come to see it as your gift. Though not an alcoholic myself, I have known many of them whom you made sober. So you keep some from ever having the addiction, and keep others from forever having it, and keep both groups from thinking that freedom from the addiction is anything but your gift.

I have heard another of your injunctions: 'Follow not your urges, but shun indulgence.' Still another thing I have heard in your Spirit, which gives me great comfort: 'What we eat will not make us better off, nor what we refrain from make us deficient'—which means that I will not be happy for what I eat, nor sad for what I do not. I also know this saying: 'I have learned to cope with what comes, familiar with plenty or privation, able to do all things in him who strengthens me.' There spoke a soldier of the celestial militia, not the kind of dust that

L1 *we are but dust]* Psalm 102.14: "Remember that we are but dust."

L2 *who was lost]* Luke 15.32: "[The prodigal son] was lost and has been found."

L8 *what pride he takes]* 1 Corinthians 1.31: "Whatever pride one takes should be taken in the Lord."

L10 *Relieve me]* Ecclesiasticus 23.6: "Relieve me of the belly's urges."

L13 *persons who are clean]* Titus 1.15: "To the clean all things are clean, to the unclean and unbelieving nothing is clean."

L14 *the person eating]* Romans 14.20: "All things are good in themselves, but he does wrong who by his diet harms another."

L16 *all things are good]* Titus 4.4: "For all things are good that you have made, and nothing is to be rejected so long as it is taken with gratitude."

L17 *diet ingratiate]* 1 Corinthians 8.8: "For diet does not ingratiate us with God."

L18 *categorize us]* Colossians 2.16: "Let no one categorize us by our food or drink."

L19 *he who eats]* Romans 14.3: "He who eats [certain foods] should not shun one who does not eat them, and he who refrains from them should not condemn the one who eats them."

L24 *knock on the door]* Revelation 3.20: "I stand at the door and knock."

L25 *Rescue me]* Psalm 17.30: "For I shall be rescued from testings."

L27 *Noah was allowed]* A list of seven different scriptural narratives involving food, to show that the kind of food is not important but the self-control exercised in its use is (*comm.*).

we are—though remember, Lord, 'we are but dust,' it was from dust that you shaped man, 'who was lost and has been found.' So Paul, too, made of dust, could not of himself say he was 'able to do all things in the one who makes me content' unless you breathed strength into him, the act that has made me love him. Strengthen me to be content in that way. Granting whatever you require, require whatever you will. Paul gives testimony to what he received from you, and 'what pride he takes is pride taken in the Lord.' A quite different voice it was, one requesting aid, that said, 'Relieve me of the belly's urges,' making it clear, God sacrosanct, that what you say should be done, can be done only by your aid.

46. It is your teaching, good Father, that 'For persons who are clean all things are clean.' Thus 'it is the person eating [not the thing eaten] who does wrong if his diet hurts another,' since 'all things are good that you have made, and nothing is to be rejected so long as it is taken with gratitude.' Nor does 'diet ingratiate us with God.' Neither should anyone 'categorize us by our food or drink.' Moreover, 'he who eats [certain foods] should not shun one who does not eat them, and he who refrains from them should not condemn the one who eats them.'

This is what you have taught about food, for which I am grateful, God my teacher, and praise you, when these words 'knock on the door' of my ears to shine light in on my heart. 'Rescue me from each of my testings.' I have no qualms about ritual uncleanness in the food, but about unclean urges toward it. I realize that Noah was allowed to eat of any food at hand, that Elijah was strengthened by meat, that [the Baptizing]

L16 *expands to your honor]* Revelation 15.4: "He will magnify your name." Augustine (T 1.1) did not think man could make God greater. Rather, we make ourselves larger in order to address his honor (*nomen*).

L18 *this world's conqueror]* John 16.33: "This world I have conquered."

L18 *interpose himself]* Romans 8.34: "At the right hand of the Father he interposes [*interpellat*] himself for us."

L19 *the weaker members]* 1 Corinthians 12.22: "Those members of the body that are weaker are also necessary."

L20 *all those written]* Psalm 138.16: "All are written in your book, though your eyes have seen my imperfection."

L22 *Smell]* This is included, though its treatment is perfunctory, just to follow the scheme of examining all his senses.

John, while supernaturally strong in his abstinence from other animals, was not ritually tainted by the locusts that were permitted him. I know as well that lentil pottage was used as a lure for Esau. David regretted his untimely thirst, and our Prince was tempted [by the devil] not with meat but bread. Thus those who made the exodus through the desert incurred blame not for wanting meat but for criticizing the Lord when he did not provide it.

47.   In the midst of such tests, then, I surely have 'trouble of the day' from my urges toward food and drink, since I cannot resolve to abstain from food once for all, never indulging in it again, as I gave up sexual intercourse. The bridle on my appetite for food must be adjusted with calibrated tightenings or loosenings of the rein, and who, my Lord, can maintain the exact degree of required tension? That is the mark of a hero, 'whose soul expands to your honor'—and I, a sinful man, am not such a person. Yet my soul, too, expands to your honor, and 'this world's conquerer' will 'interpose himself' between you and my sins, accepting me as one of 'the weaker members of his body,' one of 'all those written in your book, though you see his imperfection.'

3. The Five Senses: Smell

48.   To allurements from the sense of smell I am, for the most part, indifferent. Sweet smells I neither long for when absent nor reject when present; but I could do without them entirely, so far as I am aware. I could be wrong—knowledge of my own capacity is hidden in a murkiness I lament, and the mind,

L3 *continual testing]*   Job 7.1: "What is man's life on earth but a testing?"

L10 *when I hear music]*   Augustine's caution about church music may seem excessive, but see *comm.*

trying to estimate what it is able to do, cannot rely on itself. My inner resources are hidden from me until exposed by trial. No one should count himself safe, in a life known as 'a continual testing,' as if immune to relapse just because he has once re-formed. There is only one hope, one thing to rely on, one steady commitment to us—your pity.

4. The Five Senses: Hearing

49. I was more entangled and submissive where the plea-sures of hearing are concerned until you cut me loose and gave me back my freedom. Now when I hear music vibrant with your scripture, sung with skill in a sweet voice, I yield to some degree, I must admit, but am not hypnotized by it, since I can break off at any point. Nonetheless, when the music carries a meaning that enters into me, it makes something in my heart honor it, I know not how properly—do I prize it higher than I should? When music is added to the sacred words, I find that our souls are kindled to more ardent piety than when they stand alone, as if each emotion of our spirit were being touched by its own special tone or tune, intimately responsive to it by some secret tie. A delicious physical sound should not melt our reason, but should attend it as its subordinate partner—but once admitted on these terms, it tends to skip ahead of reason and take the lead from it. When this occurs, I go wrong without realizing it, and only recognize what has happened later on.

50. Yet at other times, suspicious of being misled, I adopt too great a caution, harshly willing to ban all melodic sweeten-ing of David's words sung in the psalms, not only from my own

L5 *the tears I shed]* After his baptism, the singing in Ambrose's Milan church moved him deeply: "How many tears I shed during the hymns and canticles, violently shaken by the voices of your church making sweet music. As those voices rinsed my ears, your truth was distilled in my heart. Religious feelings blazed within me, the tears flowed, and I found peace in them" (T 9.14).

L22 *symptom of my sins]* See *terms.*

L26 *that temple]* 1 Corinthians 3.16: "Know you not that you are God's temple?"

hearing but from that of the entire church—though I think it safer to follow a rule often reported to me as being that of Athanasius, Alexandria's bishop. He had the cantor so flatten out the tune that he seemed rather to be speaking the psalm than singing it. But in the last analysis, when I recall the tears I shed at the church music when I first returned to the faith, and how moved I am even now by the meaning of the music rather than the music itself—so long as the words are sung in a clear voice appropriately fitted to the tune—I see just how useful music can be.

So, though my mind hovers between pleasure's danger and the custom's benefits, and I would not want to adhere blindly to one view of the matter, I increasingly favor the practice of singing in church, which can strengthen the wavering soul's feeling for religion. Yet I must testify for myself that when I am moved more by the music than by its meaning, I feel this offense should be punished, and wish I had not listened to the cantor. That is my plight. Weep for it, all you whose concern for virtue issues in good works—those without that concern will not care enough to weep for me. But you, Lord my God, hear me, heed, look on with pity, and heal me, before whom I am made a riddle to myself, which is the symptom of my sins.

5. *The Five Senses: Sight*

51.   The last sense I must include in this my testimony is the sensual pleasure I derive from the body's eyes. Let the ears of 'that temple which is your people' be brotherly and devout to me as I end this account of my testing by the flesh's urges,

L1 *I groan]*   2 Corinthians 5.2: "We still groan and yearn to be covered round with our heavenly shelter."

L4 *made them firmly* [valde] *good]*   Genesis 1.31: "And God looked on everything he had made ... and all, behold, was firmly good."

L8 *empress of all colors]*   The colors have to obey light, since they emerge only at her presence, and change the instant she does.

L9 *everywhere—wherever]* Ubiubi.

L12 *to be depressed]*   A striking illustration of Augustine's Mediterranean temperament—he would have fared badly in northern gloom. He hated even Africa's winters: "Poor as I am, by general disposition and particular illness, at bearing the cold, I could not have experienced worse storms than in this miserable winter [of 411, when he was 57]" (Letter 124.1).

L14 *O Light!]*   As Augustine previously listed scriptural passages having to do with food, he now lists examples of spiritual light, to show the proper use of physical light (*comm.*). The passages referred to are Tobias 4.6, Genesis 27.1–40, and Genesis 48.10–22.

L15 *path to life]*   John 14.6: "I am path, truth, and life."

L20 *rays from his heart]*   See *comm.*

L25 *one are all those]*   John 17.22: "that all may be one."

under whose pummelings 'I groan and yearn to be covered round with my heavenly shelter.' Shapes beautiful or striking, colors bright or soft, delight my eye. I would not have them fill my soul—let God alone do that, who 'made them firmly good,' since he is my good in ways that they are not. My every waking moment, sights brush across my eyes, not intermitted as sounds are when the cantor falls silent, or the choir does. For light, the empress of all colors, floods all things visible everywhere—wherever I am in the day, wooing me with its variable coloring even when I, at my tasks, am not adverting to it. But so powerfully pervasive is this light that our impulse is to call it back if it is suddenly removed, and to be depressed if it is gone for long.

52. O Light!—that Light Tobias saw within him when, eyes blighted, he showed his son the path to life, a path he was treading beforehand, with love's feet that never strayed! O Light that Isaac beheld, with aged eyes too wearied, too outworn, to identify his sons for blessing, yet whom his blessing identified! O Light that Jacob beheld when bowed and blinded by the years! The rays from his heart shone down the generations of that people prefigured in his descendents. When his son Joseph tried to uncross the hands he laid with mystic power on his grandsons, he did not heed the outer view of Joseph, but the inner light haloing his grandsons. All those lights are one Light, and 'one are all those' who look on it with love. The physical light earlier described sweetens with a lure of danger the life of the world for lovers of the world. But those who

L1   *You All-Creating God]*   The opening words of Ambrose's most famous hymn, *Deus Creator Omnium*.

L1   *lay claim ... claimed by]*   For the play of *adsumunt ... absumuntur*. For the way Augustine goes back to singing (sound) in this section on vision (light), see *comm*.

L6   *disentangle my feet]*   Psalm 24.15: "he disentangles my feet from the snare."

L8   *You sleep not]*   Psalm 120.4: "He will not sleep, nor slumber, standing guard over Israel."

L24   *preserving their power]*   Psalm 58.10. "I shall preserve my power for you."

know how to praise light properly, 'You All-Creating God,' lay claim to the light by singing of you, and are not claimed by the dark in dreams of their own. Let me be in that choir of singers, resisting the eyes' enticements lest my feet be enmeshed as I tread your path. I lift inner eyes to you, so you may 'disentangle my feet from the snare.' You continually disentangle my feet, no matter how often I am thrashing in the snares laid about me. 'You sleep not, nor slumber, standing guard over Israel.'

53.   How many snares for the eye men contrive by ingenuity and art—dresses, shoes, vessels and other craftwork, pictures and other images, things going far beyond the norms of utility, economy, or religious symbolism. Outwardly they make idols of their own handiwork, while inwardly they unmake the handiwork they are, effacing what God fashioned in them. But these very things lead me, my God, my source of pride, to sing a hymn to you, making of praise a sacrifice to my Sacrificed One, since the work of an artist's skilled hand, made under the direction of his soul, just passes on a beauty that was shed on that soul from a source above. Toward that source my soul aspires night and day, while the creators and appreciators of art learn from above how to admire beauty rightly but not how to use it rightly. The right use is there for them to see, but they stray beyond it, not 'preserving their power for you,' but dissipating their work in pleasant trivialities. Yet even I, proclaiming and accepting these things, become at times enmeshed in beauties that I see, and you disentangle me, Lord—you do so

since I see your pity for me, yet remain pitifully enmeshed, and you in pity disentangle me, sometimes without my realizing it because though I have sometimes stumbled only slightly, I fell painfully at other times, and was thrashing in the net [when rescued].

L4 *an empty and transgressive urge*]   See *terms* and *comm*. The "eyes' urges" are obviously distinguished from trials considered under "sight" in the sequence of senses.

L12 *Hear that red*]   The twelfth use of the sequence of senses.

L13 *See how it shines*]   The thirteenth use of the sequence.

L22 *beautiful sights*]   The fourteenth use of the sequence.

V. Transgressive Knowledge (*curiositas*)

54. There is another way we can be tested, one more insidiously perilous. Beyond the cravings of the flesh, of all that delights or lures the senses, luring men far off from you to their perdition, the soul takes in through those senses an empty and transgressive urge, not to indulge the flesh but to use it in experiments rationalized in the name of mental expression or science. Since this is a craving to know, and the eyes lead the other senses in quest of knowledge, it is called in scripture 'the eyes' urges.' Though only the eye sees in a literal sense, we apply the word to the other senses when we employ them to know a thing. We do not do that with the other senses—do not say: Hear that red, or Smell that white, or Taste that glow, or Feel that brightness. We do say, however: See how it shines (which only the eyes can do). More than that, we say: See how it sounds. See how it smells. See how it tastes. See how hard it is. So all sensible knowledge is called an urge (as scripture puts it) of the eyes, since seeing, which is the prerogative of the eye, is taken as a loan word by the other senses when they, by a kind of seeing, are deployed to know.

55. This should make it easier to tell the difference between use of the senses for sensual pleasure and use of them for transgression. The former turns toward beautiful sights,

L2 *experiments with their opposites*] Augustine's first category of transgressive knowledge is the sadomasochistic, illustrated by the instance of necrophilia (*comm.*).

L3 *drive to experience and know*] This quest for a knowledge not God-oriented is exemplified in the fall of Eve (*comm.*).

L13 *arcane elements*] His second category of transgressive knowledge is the seeking of forbidden knowledge in magic and occult pursuits (*comm.*).

L16 *put God to the test*] Deuteronomy 6.16: "You shall not put to the test the Lord your God."

L17 *badgering*] *Flagitare* means "to ask with a boorish insistency."

L17 *signs and miracles*] John 4.48: "Unless you see signs and miracles, you will not believe."

L21 *God of my rescue*] Psalm 17.47: "Held on high is the God of my rescue."

L26 *indulge astrology*] Augustine earlier told how he "saw through" the claims of astrology (T 4.4–6, 7.8–10).

resonant sounds, sweet aromas, flavorful tastes, and soft touches. The latter experiments with their opposites, not submitting to ordeal for its own sake, but from the drive to experience and know. Pleasure is not exactly what one takes in the sight of a mutilated corpse, which makes men shudder—yet if one is encountered, people flock to be repelled by it and stricken pale. This is something they do not want to see [in terms of sensual pleasure] even in dreams, or if forced to look at it while awake, or if lured to the sight expecting something pretty. (The same [contrariety] can be found in the use of the other senses, though it would take time to run through them.) It is for this perverse craving that unnatural things are put on in the theater. This also leads men to pry into the arcane elements of nature, which are beyond our scope—knowing them would serve no purpose, yet men make of that knowing its own purpose. And even in real [non-magic] religion, this makes men 'put God to the test,' badgering him for 'signs and miracles' with no saving purpose, just providing excitement.

56.   In this vast forest, full of snares and perils, see how much I may have cleared and cleansed my heart of, as you gave me strength to do, 'God of my rescue.' But will I ever be confident, while so many things buzz around me in my daily life, be confident enough to claim that nothing of the sort will compel me to go view it, that I am no longer addicted to such nonsense? Admittedly, the theater no longer enchants me, nor do I indulge astrology, and I never trafficked with spirits for their knowledge—superstitious occultism I detest. Yet how many devious modes of insinuation does the Enemy use to make me

L1 *simple and unassuming . . . home of the humble*]   True religion is seen as simple when compared with the grandiosity and pretension of superstitious rites.

L5 *pray for the recovery*]   Prayer itself becomes transgressive if it seeks a magic certainty of the outcome. Augustine prays not to pray that way.

L10 *empty gossip*]   See *comm.* for the way this is transgressive knowledge, not merely trivial.

L12 *hound course a hare*]   Again, see *comm.*

L19 *hypnotized as a fly*]   Again, see *comm.*

seek a sign from you, whose service should be simple and unassuming. I beg you for the sake of our true king and our holy Jerusalem, the home of the humble, that, as I am far from consenting to such things now, I may become far and farther from it in the future. For when I pray for the recovery of some sick person, my aim is not at all for a magic cure, but that I may submit willingly to whatever you will.

57.   Who, indeed, can list all the minute and unnoticed ways by which this transgressive urge tests us daily, tripping us up? How often do we put up with empty gossip, to humor its silly bearers, only to be drawn in by the gossip as we listen? I no longer go to the arena to see a hound course a hare. But if by chance I catch sight of that in a field, the hunt attracts me, distracts my concentration on the most important matters. It reins aside not my horse's pace, but my heart's regard. I would stay stupidly rooted to the spot did you not jog me with memories of my former weakness, urging me either to use the sight as a sign of something higher leading me to you, or to brush it dismissively aside and ride on. Even sitting at home I can be hypnotized as a fly is snatched from the air by a lizard or as it blunders into a spider's web. Is the hunt any the less for the hunters' trifling size? I can, indeed, admire in them your marvelous way of ordering even slightest things—but that is not what fascinated me at first sight. And a quick recovery from that first stumble is not the same as freedom from stumbling at all. Yet I am constantly succumbing in this way, and I have no hope but your deep and deeper pity for me. My heart is a dumpster for such things, stuffed with superfluous trash, which

L15 *a mild* [lenis] *thing]*   Matthew 11.30: "My yoke is sweet, my burden light [lenis]."

often intrudes on and muddies my prayer. Even as my heart's words strain up toward your ears, my serious effort is baffled by a flood of silly thoughts flowing in from somewhere or other.

58. Should I just discount these petty things? Should they not rather drive me back to the hope I have of your pity, since you have changed so much in me already? You know what stage I am at in the changes you have worked in me. For a start, you cured me from my drive toward self-justification, as a first step toward dealing with my other sins, so you strengthen what is enfeebled, restore what is decayed, bringing pity and compassion as a crowning work, to satisfy with good things all my longings. It is for this you broke with your menaces my pride, and gentled my neck into your yoke, the yoke I bear, 'a mild thing' to me, just as you promised and as you made it (it was light all along, though I knew it not, since I shied from submitting to it).

TITLE *Worldly Designs*]   1 John 2.16: "The things of this world—the flesh's urge, the eyes' urges, and worldly designs—are not from the Father." For the translation "worldly designs," see *comm.* at **[41]**.

L1 *rule is not overweening*]   Augustine is about to examine his own record as a bishop, and the way he fails to follow the model of a ruler without pride.

L7 *rebuff the proud*]   James 4.6: "God rebuffs the proud, but sheds favor on the lowly." Behind this verse of Scripture Augustine must have remembered a famous line of his favorite poet. At *Aeneid* 6.852, Virgil described the Roman Empire's foreign policy, which was "The meek to spare, and batter down the proud."

L8 *mountains tremble*]   Psalm 17.8: "the roots of the mountains were shaken and trembled."

L11 Bravos *heaped on us*]   Psalm 39.16: "May they be instantly undone who say to me *Bravo! Bravo!*"

L12 *detaching . . . attaching*]   Play on *deponamus . . . ponamus*.

L15 *convened . . . convicted*]   Play on *concordium . . . consortium*.

L17 *set up his throne*]   Isaiah 14.13: "I shall climb above God's stars, raising up my throne . . . in the northern regions."

L17 *ice-cramped*]   See note at **[51]** for Augustine's hatred of winter.

L19 *little flock*]   Luke 12.32: "Fear not—you, the little flock—for your God will make the reign yours." The humble flock is contrasted with the proud "ice-men" aping God in the North.

VI. Worldly Designs

59.   Tell me, you whose rule is not overweening—for yours is real lordship, under no other lord—has a third kind of testing slacked off in me, or can it ever slacken? I mean my desire to be an object of others' awe and affection, for no purpose at all but to take joy in that which gives no joy. Pitiable, is it not, this filth of self-promotion? It diverts real love and untainted awe from you, who 'rebuff the proud and shed favor on the lowly,' you whose thunder strikes worldly schemes, 'makes mountains tremble to their roots.' The enemy of our true happiness uses the fact that society requires love and awe for its officers—he makes '*Bravos* heaped on us' his snares. Eagerly amassing such praise we become insensibly addicted, detaching our gratification from truth and attaching it to human flattery. It now delights us to elicit love and awe not because of you but in place of you, as the Enemy fits us to his own company, not convened with him in love but convicted with him in punishment. He has 'set up his throne in the North,' where in the dark his ice-cramped followers may bow to his crooked and misshapen aping of you. But we, Lord, are 'your little flock,' keep us yours, spread over us your wings, for us to take refuge there. Be you all our boast, all affection for us be directed at you, all awe be for your word preached by us. The man who seeks human

L4 *the sinner is praised]*   Psalm 9.24: "the sinner is praised for pleasing himself and blessed for doing evil."

L14 *oven of the tongue]*   Proverbs 27.21: "As silver in the crucible, as gold in
the furnace, so man is tested in the mouth of one praising him."

praise while you are indicting him cannot rely on those who praise for exoneration while you are judging him, nor for pardon when you are condemning him. This applies not only when 'the sinner is praised for pleasing himself or blessed for doing evil.' Even the man who is praised for some talent you bestowed on him, if he delights more in being praised for having the gift than in having the gift that is praised, he wins human praise but your indictment. And the one praising him is better than he is in being praised, since the former takes delight in a talent bestowed on a man by God, while the latter treasures being given the praise by men more than in being given the talent by you.

60.   Such testings are we put to daily, Lord, incessantly are we tested, tried day after day by 'oven of the tongue.' Here, too, when you impose self-discipline, grant whatever you require, require whatever you will. You are familiar with my heart's moaning and my eyes' flooding over this concern. I cannot judge rightly how far I am purged of this infection, since I fear that the sin has just gone into hiding, where it is visible to you but not to me. For my other ways of being tested I have found some method of self-evaluation, but not for this one. With carnal activity or a transgressive occultism, I can measure my progress in relinquishing them by the degree of anguish, greater or less, that I feel if deprived of them, whether by choice or by chance. With riches, again, which can supply means for any or all three of the sinful urges, if a man who has them cannot tell whether he is too attached to them, he can measure his detachment from them by giving them away. But how are we

to test whether we could live without praise? Clearly not by leading lives so wicked, so damned and grotesque, that anyone who knows us must revile us. What crazier ploy could be devised or adopted? If praise is customarily and rightly a concomitant of virtuous activity, it cannot be removed from what it accompanies. But if it cannot be removed, how can I test my willingness, great or little, to do without it?

61. What testimony, then, can I offer you, Lord, on this part of my testing? I can only admit that I like being praised, though I like more whatever truth there may be in the praise than the praise itself. Given the choice between being universally praised for mad and exotic behavior, or being universally denigrated for consistent and proper behavior, I am confident which I would choose. Still, I wish I were not elated by praise for good behavior—but elated I am by the tribute to good behavior, and just as dejected, I must confess, by denigration of it. And when this failing nags at me, excuses suggest themselves, how validly only you can tell, since I cannot be objective.

You have imposed on us not only self-discipline (whereby we withhold our love from certain things) but justice (whereby we confer love on proper objects), and have given as one object of such love our fellow men. Well, I often think that I am pleased at another's progress or promise when he has shown the good sense to praise me—or that I am displeased because another denigrates in me what he does not understand or what is actually laudable. Moreover, I am annoyed when another praises in me what I am not proud of, or praises inordinately what I do not consider one of my strong points. Now how am

L10 *my praise ... me ... my]* There is a pile-up of "me" words: *ME laudibus MEIS propter ME.*

L13 *mine, show me me]* Another pile-up: *deus MEUS, et ME ipsum MIHI indica.*

L20 *lure myself]* Galatians 6.3: "Whoever believes he is something, though he is nothing, lures himself into his own trap."

L21 *enacting truth]* John 3.21: "Whoever enacts the truth reaches the light."

L21 *Keep me far]* Proverbs 30.8: "Keep me far from folly and lies."

L23 *a sinner's oil]* Psalm 140.5: "Let not the oil of the sinner make heavy my head." Augustine gave the meaning of *impinguet* in *Explaining the Psalms* 140.13: "Let my head not swell with flattery."

L24 *Poor and beggarly]* Psalm 108.22: "Poor and beggarly am I."

L26 *complete what is depleted ... completion]* For the play on *de-fectus ... re-ficiatur ... per-feciatur.*

I to know whether I react this way because I insist that anyone who praises me do it on my own terms, not out of any regard for his enlightenment, or because what I like in me becomes more satisfying when others endorse that liking? In some way, then, I can accept no praise if the praiser does not share my self-image, since he is either praising what I am not proud of at all, or praising too much what I take little pride in. How can I ever be objective about myself?

62. In you, who are my truth, I acknowledge that praise should be welcomed not because it is my praise offered me for my actions, but because it edifies my neighbor. But whether I meet that standard I cannot tell, where even to know you were simpler than knowing myself. I beg you, God of mine, show me *me*, that I may testify to what I find mangled in me, and my brothers can then pray for me. Let me honestly ask myself, why, if I welcome praise only if it edifies the praiser, am I less concerned when others are falsely accused than when I am? Why do I feel more hurt if insulted myself than if I see another insulted, even if the insult is equally unjustified in either case? Is this, too, beyond my knowing? Must I conclude that I 'lure myself into my own trap' and am not 'enacting truth'? 'Keep me far from such crazed action,' Lord, let not my own self-description be 'a sinner's oil to make heavy the head.'

63. 'Poor and beggarly am I,' but better at least when recognizing this with inner sobs and seeking your pity, till you complete what is depleted in me and confirm the completion in a peace no haughty eye beholds. But every word pronounced, every act performed, before others incurs the dangerous test of

L1 *wheedling]* The endorsement (*suffragia*) is contrived (*emendicata,* O 3.237–38).

L3 *rejecting/glory . . . glories/rejection]* Chiasmus (a-b-b-a) to suggest the Catch-22 aspect of pride, the impossibility of escaping its way of coiling about itself.

L6 *vain of nothing]* If one achieves freedom from dependence on others' praise, that can reflect an even deeper pride, satisfied with no approval but one's own. And this takes three forms: (1) denying that any good in oneself is God's gift, or (2) admitting it is his gift , but thinking one deserves it, or (3) giving God credit for it but not sharing its benefits with others (to avoid dependence on them).

wooing praise, wheedling a coaxed endorsement of one's self-estimate. Overcoming this test becomes a new form of test—to glory vainly in rejection of vainglory, for one is not rejecting the glory if one glories in the rejection.

64. Inward, deeper in, there lies a variant on this temptation, whereby people are vain of nothing but their own approval, whether others approve of them or no, not even trying to win their approval. But you profoundly disapprove of self-approvers—they count as a distinction what disfavors them; or count real distinctions as their own, not as coming from you; or count them as coming from you, but by their own desert; or count them as your gift, yet not as something to be enjoyed with others, but to be withheld from them. You observe how my heart trembles at all three prospects, and all similar perils and toils. And I realize that I have not so much stopped wounding myself as you have not stopped healing me over again.

L7 *proceeded . . . receding]*   For the play on *ingressus . . . recessus.*

L9 *pondered it]*   Habakuk 3.2: "I pondered your works and trembled."

VII. Conclusion

65. Where, my God, my Truth, have I ever wandered without your being there with me, to teach me what I should shun, what seek—whenever, at least, I took my own faulty perceptions to you for correction? I have surveyed what my senses could of the outer world. Those senses themselves, and the body that feels them, and the life that moves the body, I have observed in myself. After that, I proceeded down receding depths of memory, their complicated vastness, mysteriously crammed with riches beyond counting—'I pondered it, and trembled'—and nothing could I have known of this without you, though nothing of it was you. Nor could I, who did the searching, be you. I ran through it all, trying to inventory each item and assign it its proper worth. I assessed the reports brought in from my senses (though some things were mingled with matter from my internal inventory) and I distinguished and numbered which sense was bringing what report. Making a survey of this rich store, some things I deposited there, and some withdrew. In all this activity, I—or, rather, the faculty by which I did it—was not you, for you are the light everlasting which I turned to for seeing whether and what each thing was, and what it was worth. You were what I heard teaching and guiding, as I often do—it is my comfort, and to it I resort,

L3 *scattered selves . . . exile]* Isaiah 11.12: "He will bring Israel's exiles home, Israel's scattered he will reunite." Augustine thinks of his disparate elements as a kind of internal diaspora, an exile from himself that God will bring to an end on the model of Israel's return to itself.

L5 *made complete]* The ecstatic moment is not made stable on earth—a bafflement he experienced with the fleeting glimpse of divinity he shared with Monnica at T 9.25: "If this were made constant . . . would that not be what is meant by the words, 'Enter the joy of your God'?—a joy that will be ours when?—only when all things rise ('though not all are changed')."

L9 *compulsion's heavy baggage]* Compulsion *(consuetudo)* is a chain at T 8.10, defeating freedom of the will.

L16 *hurled off]* Psalm 30.23: "I said in my seizure that I am hurled off from the gaze of your eyes."

L23 *What forms]* Literally, "by what rites [*sacramentis*]." But he is mocking the ritual formalities of those seeking occult knowledge, as at [55–56].

whenever I can, from the press of affairs. Nor in all these things that I look at (in your light) do I find secure refuge but in you. In you my 'scattered selves are reunited,' not to be 'parted in exile' from you. At times you admit me into feelings of deep sweetness, honeyed I know not how, which, were they made complete, would make this life something beyond this life. But then I am toppled back to earth, weighted with heavy burdens, plunged into compelled ways, netted, wailing strongly but strongly netted still. So great is compulsion's heavy baggage. Here, I can abide but do not wish to; there, I wish to abide but cannot—miserable either way.

66.   I have performed an examination of the symptoms left in me by sin, conducting it under the heading of the three urges, and I have called your right arm to my rescue; for even with a wounded heart I recognized your splendor. Stricken down, I asked: Can anyone strive upward? 'I am hurled off from the gaze of your eyes.' You are the truth ruling all things, yet I, while greedy not to lose you, wanted to have you and keep my own lies too—much as the liar does not want to lie so well as not to recognize the truth himself. That is why I lost you, who will not share your habitation with a lie.

67.   Who will help me to rejoin you? Should I employ angelic agencies? If so, by what approach? What forms should I submit? Many, of whom I have heard reports, have tried this, who wanted to return to you but felt unable to do it themselves. Addicted to the lure of occult visions, they met only with delusion. Lifted up by pride in their learning, with swelled

L3 *masters of this lower air*]   Ephesians 2.2: "the prince of the power of this [lower] air."

L5 *changeling*]   2 Corinthians 11.14: "Satan has power to become a change-ling into an angel of light."

L17 *wage paid*]   Romans 6.23: "The wage paid for sinning is death." A *stipendium* was the wage paid for working, especially a soldier's work for military service. Since Augustine counts the death of the soul deprived of God as real death, Satan is subject to death even though he lacks a mortal body.

L22 *mediating*]   1 Timothy 2.5: "As there is one God, so there is one mediator between God and man, the man Christ Jesus."

chest rather than humbly beaten breast, they fell in with comrades of a similar disposition, fellow conspirators in pride—'the masters of this lower air'—who befuddled them with black arts in their quest for a purifying mediator, who was not to be found there. Their mediator was the devil, that 'changeling into an angel of light,' whose incorporeal state had a potent charm over their proud corporality. They were mortal and sinning, where you Lord, to whom they were haughtily seeking reunion, are immortal and sinless. A mediator between God and man should be in some way like God, in some way like men, lest in these two respects he should be similar to men but far from God, or similar to God and far from men, and fail to be their meeting point. That false mediator, whose pride was rightly misled by your hidden judgment, does have one thing in common with men—sin—and would like to be seen as having one thing, too, in common with God: he pretends to immortality because he is not clothed in mortal flesh. But since 'the wage paid for sinning is death,' he is like men in this as well, and is condemned to death.

68. The true mediator, revealed to us only by the secret of your pity, and sent to teach us lowliness by example, is 'Christ Jesus, mediating between God and men'—placed between mortal sinners and the immortal innocent, mortal with men, innocent with God. By the justice linking him to God, he can give to sinners, linked to him by redemption, a reprieve from the death that he willingly shared with them, since the wage paid to innocence is life and peace. He was revealed to the holy men of antiquity, so they could be saved by faith in his suffering to

L2 *mediator in terms of likeness]* Augustine thought of the Incarnation (more than of the crucifixion) as the saving act of God, since it restored the harmony between God and man that had been broken by Adam.

L3 *God in company]* John 1.1: "and the Word was in God's company."

L5 *not sparing]* Romans 8.32: "He did not spare his Son, but gave him over for all of us."

L8 *equality with you]* Philippians 2.6–8: "Who, being of God's rank, did not think equality with God a usurpation . . . [but] became obedient to the point of dying, dying even on a cross."

L9 *free man]* Psalm 87.5–6: "I am a man with no supporters, free among mortals."

L10 *power to lay down]* John 10.17: "I lay down my life and I shall lift it up again."

L13 *servants become sons]* Galatians 4.7: "You are no longer a servant but a son."

L14 *heal all symptoms]* Psalm 102.3: "healing all sin's symptoms."

L15 *who sits]* Romans 8.34: "Christ Jesus . . . is at God's right hand and he interposes himself for us."

L20 *become flesh]* John 1.14: "The Word became flesh and took up his dwelling with us."

L24 *This is the reason]* 2 Corinthians 5.15: "This is the reason Christ died and rose, that he who lives should no longer live in himself, but in him who died for us all."

L27 *throw all my worry]* Psalm 54.23: "Throw all your worry over to the Lord, he will will nurture you."

L27 *live in wonder]* Psalm 118.18: "I will live in wonder at your scripture."

L28 *My 'ignorance]* Psalm 68.6: "God, you are familiar with my ignorance, and my sins are not hidden from you."

come, as we are redeemed by faith in his sufferings undergone. He is our mediator in terms of likeness as a man, but not as the Word of God, who is equal (not like) to God—he is 'God in company with God,' though there is only one God.

69. What love you bore us, best of fathers, in 'not sparing your only son, but giving him over for us,' the sinful! What love you bore us, since for our sake, though 'he did not think equality with you a usurpation, he became obedient even to the point of dying on a cross.' As the only 'free man among mortals,' who had 'power to lay down his life and to lift it up again,' he became both victor and victim for us, victor because victim, both priest and sacrifice for us, priest because sacrifice, making your 'servants become sons,' because he is both son to you and servant to us. My hope in him is not empty, since you will 'heal all symptoms left by my sins,' through him 'who sits at your right hand and interposes himself for us'—without whom I had despaired, since sin's symptoms in me are many, many and severe, but stronger is your medicine than they. We might have taken the word of God to be too far above us for any traffic with men, and been without hope for ourselves, had he not 'become flesh and taken up his dwelling with us.'

70. Ground down by my sins and by the weight of my sorrow, I troubled my heart with thought of escape into the desert, but you forbade it and strengthened me by saying: 'This is the reason Christ died for all, that those who live should no longer live in themselves but in him who died for them.' So now, Lord, see how 'I throw all my worry over to you,' to 'live in wonder at your scripture.' My 'ignorance and sins you

l2 *with his blood]* Revelation 5.9: "You have bought us for God by your blood."

l3 *secreted all riches]* Colossians 2.3: "[in] whom are secreted all the treasures of wisdom and knowledge."

l6 *are filled]* Psalm 21.27: "The poor will eat and be filled."

l7 *quest of the Lord]* Psalm 21.27: "Those in quest of the Lord shall praise him."

are familiar with,' but teach me and heal. It was your only-begotten son who 'bought me with his blood,' and 'in him are secreted all riches of wisdom and knowledge.' Let no haughty ones crow over me, since I know at what cost I was purchased—I eat it, drink it, give it out, and want in my neediness to be filled with it, among those who 'eat and are filled,' since 'those in quest of the Lord shall praise him.'

PART III

Commentary

I. Why Should Others Overhear Me?

Augustine's introductory section has four aims:

1. *To move from the past to the present.* After nine books devoted to his past life, before the victory of grace in his soul, Augustine assesses his current condition. He means by the present his life after baptism **[4]**. He extended the narrative of his life just a few months beyond his baptism, which allowed him to close off his earlier days with the death of his mother. The description of his mystical conversation with her in effect shows the new phase of life opened to him by his baptism. The decade between Monnica's death and his time of writing *The Testimony* is therefore not included in what he calls the account "in sequence" of the first nine books (T 11.1).

We would like to hear about the decade that preceded his writing of *The Testimony*, since it included his call to the priesthood by popular acclamation, his promotion to bishop, and his busy literary career. But he does not want to talk to God about these external events. They are not like his winding journey toward baptism. Now, that goal arrived at, he is just a Christian among Christians. His testimony will be a report on his internal aspirations, his gratitude for graces given, his penitence at graces resisted, and the truths of Scripture he is studying and praying to understand. This book is therefore the hinge between the first nine books, with a narrative structure, and the last three books, with their structure by subject (Book Eleven devoted to the Father, Book Twelve to the Son, and Book Thirteen to the Holy Spirit. This intervening book is a preparation for studying the Trinity, a purification of his mind and senses, and a plea for enlightenment.

2. *To pray for honesty in his self-assessment.* Unless God helps Augustine be entirely candid about what he owes to his graces, and how in many ways he continues to fail him, this testimony will be an affront to the truth that God *is*. "I would be sealing you off from me, not me from you" **[2]**. He investigates his motives **[4]** before turning to the motives of his readers **[5]**. Which means he must advert to his readers in a formal way, not merely incidentally.

3. *To explain why he lets others overhear him.* The whole *Testimony* is a prayer addressed to an audience of one. But he is publishing this prayer, which brings readers into this most intimate of books. Augustine had addressed in *The Teacher* (2) the apparent anomaly that prayer is a private matter, but one that can be conducted in public, especially by priests who lead the community's prayers: "Talking is not needed for praying— unless, of course, priests talk, to signal outward their interior message; not that God should hear, but that men should, who, when they hear, are jointly reminded of their dependence on God." He does not, in this book, have the excuse of leading liturgical prayer. This is a very private exercise. Nonetheless, people of goodwill have asked him to describe his life with God **[4]**, and he can do so on two grounds—to solicit their prayers

for him in his failures, and to share gratitude with them for God's graces when he does not fail [5].

4. *To interpret his hearers' motives.* Since others cannot directly know Augustine's interior state, which is beyond their observation, they must take his word for what he tells them. There is no scientific basis for their doing this, since he is obviously a biased observer. They can only believe, not know—and the grounds for that are not his own veracity but their own love. They are disposed to recognize God's activity in others, by a fellowship of the baptized. They read his soul in the light of their own souls' traffic with the Spirit. As Paulinus of Nola wrote to Augustine's friend, Alypius: "As he [God] knew us before and wrought us to will the same things, in a unity of belief or a belief in unity, so we are linked by a love that comes before our meeting, recognizing each other not by physical presence but as shown to each other in the Spirit." This letter is in Augustine's collection (Letter 24) because Paulinus was also asking Augustine (Letter 25) for an account of Alypius's spiritual journey. Pierre Courcelle thought that this correspondence (of the year 494) prompted the whole idea of *The Testimony*, which was begun within a few years from its date. O'Donnell thinks that this is too simplistic a view of *The Testimony*'s multiple motivations (O 2.358–60), but he admits it may have been a contributing factor, citing [4] (O 3.162). In any event, the Paulinus letter expresses the spirit in which Augustine hoped to be read, and his reason for letting others overhear his prayer.

II. The Current Search for God

In the project of assessing himself, as a preparation for the
study of the Trinity that is coming up, Augustine runs through
a kind of "program analysis" on the state of his soul, like a
pilot's list of things to be checked before takeoff. He will assess his relation to his own five senses, to the four elements
of the created world, to the three urges (*concupiscentiae*) of
1 John 2.16, to the four excitements (*perturbationes*) of the
soul, to the three times of memory (past, present, future). If
this looks mechanical, its note of method comes from the as-
cetical discipline required for the ascent of the mind to God. A
labor of purification must precede the entrance into mystery.

8.   In this limbering up of the soul's powers, no list is used
more than that of the five senses. These are usually listed in
what O'Donnell calls "the sequence of senses," an order based
on the presumed nobility of each sense. Sight comes first (as
the sense linked most extensively with knowing), then (in
descending order) hearing, smell, taste, and touch. (He will
reverse the list, making it in ascending order, in his most exten-
sive testing of himself sense by sense at [41–53].)

In trying to rise above the senses, Augustine is not rejecting their importance or usefulness. They too testify to God, and he will seek their internal analogues in his attempts to describe his relation to God. The impression that Augustine was puritanical or pessimistic about creation is confuted by his many rhapsodic descriptions of the world's sensuous beauty. In the early flush of his conversion he had written against the senses in his *Answer to the Skeptics* 1.3, but he rebuked himself for doing this in his *Reconsiderations* (1.1.2), where he notes the existence of the "spiritual senses" described here. The analogy with the body's senses could not be valid unless the latter had a nobility that could be further ennobled. He often stresses the body's exquisite attunement to the world's allurements, a perfection of the responding instrument that is clearly a crowning achievement of the Creator. It is this exquisite fit with physical beauty that makes these senses a useful indication of the way the soul will be fitted to God:

> The beauty of physical things is appealing (gold, silver, and the rest), and we sway in response to what touches the flesh or affects any of the senses by its fitness to them. Our life in this world is tempting because it accommodates us to its order, patterned to beautiful (if lower) things (T 2.10).

Augustine was an extraordinarily sensuous thinker. His vivid imagery often turns to internal sense organs: the heart or soul has a mouth to taste the Lord, a nose to catch the perfume of his presence, an ear to hear him, a tongue to address him. There is nothing mechanical about his first four run-throughs of the sequence of senses, all four contained in this passage, where the list is artfully varied in each of its uses:

> What, in loving you, do I find lovable? Not, surely, physical splendor, nor time's orderliness—not light's clarity (how kindly its aptness to the eye), nor sweet linkages of variable melody; not the soft fragrances of flower, oil, or spice; not honey or heaven-bread; not limbs that intermingle in embrace—these are not what, in loving you, I love. And yet I do—*do* love a kind of light, a kind of song or fragrance, food or embrace—in loving you, who are my light and voice and fragrance and food and embrace, all of them deep within me, where is my soul's light that fades not, its song that ends not, a fragrance not dispersed in air, a taste never blunted with satiety, an embrace not ending in depletion. This is what, in loving my God, I love **[8]**.

He introduces the first use of the list with two things to indicate the sensible world in general—materiality and change: "physical splendor and time's orderliness." Change is often the soul's enemy in Augustine; but here he refers to time's *decus* to show how good is everything as God created it.

The four lists of the senses, which follow, are arranged in a kind of chiasmus (a-b-b-a): mere lists of nouns in the middle two sections, and expanded descriptions in the outer sections. The physical world is the subject of a-b (description, then mere listing), the internal world of b-a (the list, then the description). The chiastic, or interlocking, order is often used to suggest a dialectical relation of its members in Augustine. Here it shows that even in transcending the senses, one must use them, since the spiritual senses are in continual interplay with the physical ones.

9.   Another checklist is gone through, that of the four elements that make up creation. Augustine questions each in turn, this time moving *up* a scale of increasing dignity and decreasing weightiness, earth on the bottom, fire on top. Fire is represented by the stars, which are "ramparts of fire around our world," as Lucretius put it (*flammantia moenia mundi*, 1.73)—a verse Augustine knew and referred to at *The Trinity* (4. Preface). The senses' interrogation of the four eminent representatives of the elements is a kindred form of address, since Augustine thought his own body was made up by a "tempering" of the same four elements, and that his body's "natural place" in the cosmos was fixed by the weight of this compound (*Explaining the Psalms* 29.2.10).

10.–11.   Augustine now distinguishes between the way animals respond to their senses and the way man does. Animals are in many ways more acute, with a better sense of smell or sight or hearing according to their species. But they cannot refer what they pick up to an internal seat of judgment to ask the sensed things questions about God. Augustine wants now to question that internal judge (and not simply the external things it has been judging)—and this takes him inward toward his own memory. Everything so far in Book Ten has been a launching pad to rocket him into the "inner space" of memory.

III. The Contents of Memory

1. *Representations* (imagines)

12.   The soul as mind takes from sensible experience representations of what has been experienced. These representations
are not visual images, since the experiences are too complex to
be captured in anything so static or single as an "image" as we
use that term. Besides, the mind works with the representations as so much raw material for refashioning ("by expanding, contracting, or otherwise manipulating them"). Thus we
must not treat this category of memories as sealed off from the
ones treated later. There is cross-contamination of the things,
though they are clearly non-identical. Thus, numbered numbers and numbering numbers are different, one derived from
the senses, one from reason; but they can reinforce or confuse
each other in the endless activity of memory.

13.   Despite the combinative powers of the memory, Augustine is fascinated by the fact that mental representations
of sensation, which more resemble mind than they do the
outside occasions for their formation, do not "bleed" into
each other in the medium of mind. Red is never reducible
to loud or soft. Touch is never heard—when the two occur
in conjunction, they preserve their distinctiveness. They can

be juxtaposed with each other but never dissolved into each other. This is an example of Augustine's close observation of memory's behavior.

14. For memory's power to construct more complex representations out of simpler ones, see Introduction 2. The predictive power of the mind is developed further at T 11.24–25. The power of the memory to contain vast things is a mark of the creative power of representation, which can re-present things in their proper scale without taking up any space at all.

15. The paradoxes of man reflect the paradoxes of God. "The mind is too limited to contain itself—yet where could the uncontained part of itself be?" He had asked of God at T 1.3:

> Since, then, you fill heaven and earth, do they contain you? Or do you fill them, with a surplus of you left over, beyond their containing? Then where, once heaven and earth are filled, does the overflow of you go? Do you, who contain all things, need no container because what you fill is filled by your containing *it*?

2. *Rules* (percepta)

16. The next step up from sensible representations in the memory takes Augustine to the "rules of art" in liberal studies. These were very important to Augustine, since he had been a teacher of the liberal arts and a practitioner of the art of rhetoric. Even more important, the liberal arts were thought of by Neoplatonists of his time as conditioners of the soul, teach-

ing it to withdraw from the senses into a realm of purer knowledge. In his early days as a Christian, Augustine had planned to write treatises on each of the liberal arts, as a method of religious *askēsis*—a project broken off only when he was called to the priesthood by the congregation in Hippo. The benefit of the liberal arts, he said while preparing for baptism, is that they are a means of "moving off from the senses, drawing the soul in upon itself, and holding it as thing apart" (*Order in the Universe* 1.3).

In one of the treatises he did begin and bring some way to completion, *Music*, he admits that the rules of rhythm take one only partway toward the pure sphere of mind, but that is an important first step. He expresses a hope (6.1) that "the reader will understand that this lowly road is not of lowly value—it is, in fact, the one I have trudged along with those sharing my weakness (since I am no athlete of the mind), rather than commit unfledged wings at once to thin air."

Why did he consider liberal studies a way of escaping the sensible world? There were seven such studies (*disciplinae*), a "set of three" (*trivium*) and a "set of four" (*quadrivium*). The *trivium* had to do with language (grammar, logic, rhetoric). The *quadrivium* dealt with number (geometry, arithmetic, music, astronomy). The first set was less exalted above the sensible than the second set. In fact, we may ask how language can be considered apart from the sounds made by the sensible tongue for the sensible ear. To understand Augustine's position we must go back to his dialogue with his son, *The Teacher*, where he says that people are not taught language. The meaning of words in a specific language is indeed discovered with the help of others—they will point, for instance, to a head and say that is what is referred to in Latin as *caput*. It would be a different word if one were learning Greek (*kephalē*), but the same meaning would be involved, and one acquires that meaning by looking with one's own eyes at the real head. But "in a space more remote from my exterior" the rules of language are not taught by anything external to the mind. They are, as Noam Chomsky thinks, inborn. They are simply the way the mind works—by God's direct illumination of the soul (according to Augustine) or as the result of evolution (according to Chomskyans— though Chomsky himself expressed some reservations about that explanation).

The rules of logic and rhetoric are extensions or variants on the rules of language, so one does not learn these, either, from the senses. Augustine spells out his meaning more extensively at **[30]**, where he distinguishes knowledge of the rules of persuasion from (a) those who know what the word refers to but do not understand its rules, and (b) those who observe with their senses the effect of persuasion and wish they had the art. At T 8.13, he refers to his earlier false position as a teacher of persuasion, since that cannot be taught. He tells his son what he conceives to be the real relation of teacher to pupil when it comes to the liberal arts:

What father sends a child to school with the silly aim of finding out what the teacher's understanding is? Rather, when all subjects, even those concerning virtue and wisdom, have been expounded by those who profess them, then students, if they are really to be called that, investigate within themselves whether what they are hearing is true, strenuously putting it to the test of their own interior truth. That is the point at which they learn. And when they reach an inner conviction of truth, they praise their teachers, not realizing that, even if the teachers knew what they were saying, the praise rightly belongs to the taught ones not the ones who taught. Men make the mistake of calling others their teachers when they are no such thing, since there is a near-simultaneity between what is said and what is understood, and where inner assent follows so quickly on outer discussion, they think the latter caused the former (*The Teacher* 45).

17.   Augustine does not pretend to explain how things like the rules of language come to be in the memory. They were not always present in their fully formed state. Given the occasion to advert to them, he has to test them, "establishing their truth" within himself before he can confidently file them away for use. Others may have called his attention to them, but it was his own attention that made him accept them. There came a moment of instant recognition—"Of course, it must be so"— but only after he had worked the matter out for himself.

It is often claimed that Augustine had a Platonic concept of *anamnesis,* by which we remember things known in a previous existence. That is one of many possibilities Augustine entertains without reaching a clear decision about it. If there is any truth to the matter, he felt, it was less a matter of individual pre-existence than a previous solidarity in Adam. But he felt no need to solve a mystery so long as one can reach the truths important for practical use—in this case, the conclusion that such knowledge *is* inborn, and that God is responsible for its being so. How God brought this about is not clear. The inborn truths, though they make their presence felt, do not explain their own presence: "Let them tell me, if they can, how they came to be inside me. . . . It stumps me." He thought it a duty to remain agnostic where evidence did not justify a clear judgment. On the origin of the soul, he often said, he remained uncertain: "When a thing obscure in itself defeats our capacity, and nothing in scripture comes to our aid, it is not safe for humans to presume they can pronounce on it" (Letter 190.5).

18.   The three questions Augustine refers to in the first sentence of this paragraph we would more naturally think of as philosophical, not rhetorical. By doing so we miss the importance of rhetoric as an intellectual discipline in Augustine's time. According to Aristotle, the art of persuasion depends in large part on the evaluation and presentation of evidence, making it closely associated with logic—Aristotle calls the two arts "dance partners" (*Rhetoric* 1354a). For the question whether a thing exists, see Cicero, *Topica* 4.26–27. An application of the problem is in Pseudo-Cicero, *Address to Herennius* 5.8— which advocates establishing whether a crime exists by testing for signs of it by each of the five senses. For essence and accidents as rhetorical categories, see Aristotle, *Topica* 101b–102a.

The way the rules of rhetoric are found in the memory is described in this paragraph. The mind puts together elements that were already in the memory, but were disconnected there until thought imposed order on them—and even then they must be held together by continued attention or they tend to come apart again and slide off into their separated elements. (Augustine modestly began this section—at [16]—by saying he was discussing those rules of the liberal studies that he had not forgotten, a major admission from a former professional in those studies.) Here Augustine derives the meaning of *cogitare* ("to think") from *cogere* ("to force together"). I use the term "express," for pressing together, to give a sense of the etymological play with other terms in this passage. To express the truth is to bring together its elements in a coherent and manageable way, for future use and preservation. Arguments from the shared etymology of words were far more common and respected in antiquity than today. Cicero called this the art of "linked things," *conjugata* (*Topica* 3.12).

3. *Axioms* (rationes)

19. We move now from the *trivium* (language) to the *quadrivium* (number), whose axioms and applications (*leges*) are even less connected with the senses than are the rules of language. Number was considered a mental purifier from at least the time of Pythagoras, and Augustine relied on this notion in his early treatise *Music,* where (6.58) number orders the music of the spheres. One of the foundational texts of *The*

Testimony is Wisdom 21.21: "You have ordered all things in measure *and number* and weight" (emphasis added). There is a number mysticism in much of his exegesis of Scripture.

The presence of number in the memory is thus, for Augustine, an important indication of the soul's link with divinity. Number is generative. It has a multiplier effect (*multiplicitas*) in its capacity to be extended into endless theorems in many fields, or to be applied to numerable situations that it orders without being enmeshed in their materiality. Augustine makes this an argument against philosophical materialism, the doctrine of those who mock spiritual realities at the end of this paragraph.

20. The rigor of the mathematical sciences has to be worked through again and again. Augustine remembers arguments he found fallacious, and his memory of the arguments is true even if the arguments were not—a version of his claim, in various places, that "even if I am in error, it is true that I have to exist in order to be making the error" (*Truth in Religion* 73; *The Trinity* 10.14, 15.21). In its most famous form—*Si enim fallor, sum*, "Even if I am in error, I *am*" (*The City of God* 11.26)—this has often been compared to the Descartes dictum *Si cogito, sum*. But Descartes based a whole epistemology on his statement, using it establish other truth claims. Augustine is more interested in the continuity with himself in memory, with personal identity. For what other things we can know, Augustine was often more skeptical than Descartes. As Christopher Kirwan writes (in *Augustine*, 1989, p. 33):

Augustine claims in the *Contra Academicos* to have found a range of propositions that can be known. But unlike Descartes he does not seek to build any edifice on this foundation: in particular he does not seek to reinstate the multitudinous propositions which pass for known in scholarly circles, let alone in ordinary life.

4. *Reactions* (affectiones)

21. The first thing that impresses Augustine about remembering the souls' reactions is that, once lodged in memory, these reactions are at a remove from their occasion. The reaction is recalled without being re-enacted. The memory contains two times held simultaneously—the time when I was angry, and the time when I can recall that experience without repeating it. There is the *affectio* that responds to the *perturbatio*, and then there is the *affectio* recalled without the *perturbatio*. This discontinuity suggests to Augustine the "undignified" comparison to eating and digesting. The *affectio* still tastes the *perturbatio* when it first occurs. But it no longer tastes it when it has gone into the "belly" of memory. Of course, one can renew one's anger while recalling it—but there will still be two times in play, since the renewed anger is colored by all the things that have happened to the soul since its first arousal, things that can increase, lessen, or otherwise alter the *affectio*. So there are still two times being presented.

22. Augustine remembers not only sensible experience and the liberal studies, but his reactions to the four excitements

(*perturbationes*) of Stoic doctrine. The excitements move Augustine—he makes no claim to the Stoic imperturbability (*apatheia*). But the soul itself acts under the provocation of the excitement. It is *re*-acting, but still acting. The soul is never, in Augustine, a mere passive register of things happening to it. It either makes trouble for itself when acting alone or fulfills itself by acting in cooperation with grace.

The idea of *decanting* things from memory (*depromi*) shows how Augustine's language is affected by surrounding imagery (in this case, the preceding idea of the memory as a stomach and the the following idea of recalling as belching, to be savored in "the mind's mouth"). Carrying wine is a Horatian topos. Augustine wrote to Simplician, the priest (later bishop) who affected his conversion: "The paternal reaction of your gracious heart is not a new and untried vintage to me, but a tried and trusted one I taste again" (Letters 37.1). He even quotes Horace (*Epistles* 1.2.69–70) on the way a vessel "remembers" wine it once held:

> A cask's first wine, into it fit,
> Long afterward will breathe of it.

Augustine says we must not push the analogy between memory and the mind's belly to the point where recalling by memory resembles recalling by belching—since the latter *does* involve tasting all over again. In a move typical of his rhetorical strategies, Augustine highlights the mystery of the self by an outlandish comparison, and then deepens the mystery by saying it goes beyond even the outlandish comparison. (See, for instance, the mystery of how we "face ourselves" in the mind at T 8.16 (see Introduction 3).

23. The mystery of recallable anger is that it is something more intimate to me than remembering the sun, yet somehow not as directly accessed. Our representation of the sun is not a representation of a representation of the sun, or of a word for the sun, but of the sun itself. But our reaction to the excitement of anger is more detachable from its object than is sensible perception. Nonetheless, it is a memory of *me*, not of something other than I am. Does that give me a kind of immediate access, like the one I have to number? Augustine, as he often does, leaves the puzzle unsolved. This is one of those two-edged aspects of the self to which Augustine was ever alert. On the one hand, we transcend our original reaction by remembering it without the excitement; on the other hand, this seems to make us less directly related to ourselves than to number (present in memory directly) or to sensible perception (present in memory by representation). Thus memory *does* give some degree of *apatheia* when we remember our reaction the second time around. The original anger had a great "taste of self" in it that we can renounce in memory. The whole early part of *The Testimony* is thus a recollection of sin performed in order for Augustine to separate himself from it, achieving a self by renouncing a self. The memory of one's own reactions exists in some mysterious region apart from the direct representation of sensible objects and the direct apprehension of mathematical truths. Self-knowledge is to that extent self-estrangement.

5. *Forgetting* (oblivio)

24.   If reactions to excitements present a puzzle in the way they are remembered, that is as nothing to what Augustine explores next—the memory of forgetting. I already discussed (Introduction 1) the kinetic way Augustine conceives this problem. It is as a motion disturbed that we feel the loss of something we "moved with" before [28].

25.   Augustine has used the imagery of an "interior landscape" for his self/memory throughout this book. This is the most striking use of that image. He is an Adam condemned to work the hard resisting soil of the post-lapsarian world—and he is both the worker of that soil and the soil itself.

26.   His *aporia* (paralysis) makes him try to break off his nagging at the question of *oblivio*. Having reached no sure answer to the problem he has set himself, he decides to leave memory entirely and seek God outside it. But that proves an impossibility, as he will admit at the end of his discussion of memory [35-38]. In fact, the mere attempt to go outside memory makes him realize that he has to remember what he is seeking outside memory. How does he know what he is looking for? His attempt to escape memory is beaten back. It is one of the never-ending satisfactions of *The Testimony* that Augustine does not simply describe what is happening to him, but *enacts* it before our eyes. There is a comic aspect to the turn of events in this paragraph. Having complained that he cannot

understand how he remembers forgetting, he cannot now forget forgetting!

27. Which brings him to the woman of Luke 15.8, who knows what she is looking for. This and the next paragraph mark a transition into the subject of happiness, which all men are looking for. But how will they recognize it? It is not like the coin lost by the woman. She had possessed it, seen it, held it in her hand. Why do we all know that we are looking for happiness, though we have never had such clear prior possession of it?

6. *Happiness* (beata vita)

29. The universal instinct for a happiness we have not fully experienced is deftly analyzed by Augustine. Chesterton said that we tend to call this an odd world, though it is the only one we know. This is akin to Augustine's discussion of the experience of remembering that we forgot, which is almost like sensation in a lost limb. We feel that we need something for our completion. Every home just reminds us of our "real" home which we have never seen. As Chesterton put it in *Orthodoxy* (Doubleday, 2001, pp. 51, 167):

This is the prime paradox of our religion: something that we have never in any full sense known is not only better than ourselves, but even more natural to us. . . . We have all forgotten what we really are. All that we call common sense and rationality and practicality and positivism only means that for certain dead levels of our life we forget that we have forgotten. All that we call spirit and art and ecstasy only means that for one awful instant we remember that we forget.

30.　Augustine tried to "place" the memory of happiness by contrasting it with the other categories of remembered things he has been treating. It is not like remembering a sensible object (Carthage). It is not like remembering the truths of the *quadrivium* (numbers). It is not like remembering the truths of the *trivium* (the art of persuasion). This last category deserves a second look, since everyone would like to be persuasive, for at least some purposes. But we have seen persuasive persons, so we know concretely what the word "persuasion" means, and we can wish, on that basis, that we had the art even though we do not know its rules—none of which is true of happiness.

7. *God* (Deus)

38.　Augustine closes the long section on memory with this justly famous short paragraph, which brings back the sequence of senses (making a tenth time for the book so far) in their spiritual counterparts first mentioned in [8]. Far from mechanical, this use of the sensual inventory reaches a climax of yearning for inner satisfaction of so thorough a sort that sensual overload is merely an approximation to the reality. The anchoring of these refined sensations "within" is accomplished by a characteristic expression: "You were waiting within me while I went outside me. . . ." The paradox of being outside one's own self, of going farther from God by leaving oneself, is one of Augustine's basic insights. "You were more inward to me than I was to myself" (*interior intimo meo*, T 3.11). "He was inside, I outside, myself" (T 7.11). "They strive to travel outward, deserting what is within themselves, where God is within the within" (*interiora . . . interior, The Trinity* 8.7.11).

IV. The Flesh's Urges

39.   This paragraph marks the transition from the search through memory to the use of memory for self-examination, giving the report on his soul's condition promised at the outset. Like any good rhetorician, Augustine begins with an admission of the difficulties of his task.

40.   The Christian perfectionist Pelagius (floruit 305–418) began what became a long-drawn-out war between his followers and Augustine when he heard this paragraph read to him. Augustine, who refers to the episode repeatedly, gave the fullest account of its relation to *The Testimony* in his late work, *The Gift of Sustaining Faith* 20.53:

> Which of my books has become more often and favorably read than *The Testimony*, which I issued before the Pelagian heresy arose? It is true that I said in it—and said frequently [four times]—"Granting whatever you request, request whatever you will." When these words were read to Pelagius by a friend of mine (and my fellow bishop) who was staying with him, Pelagius could not contain himself. Attacking the sentence with some passion, he all but treated his visitor as his adversary. Yet what does God first and foremost require but that we should

believe in him? And this belief is what he himself grants if it is proper to say, "Granting whatever you request." In that book, which told the story of my conversion—of God's converting me to the very faith that I had trashed with my sad mad babblings—you recall, do you not, that I told how I was won by the faithful and daily tears of my mother, praying that I should not perish? I thus made the point that God by his grace can convert men's wills not only when are turned away from the true faith but when they are directed against that faith.

Pelagius felt that forever waiting on grace was just an excuse for not taking charge of one's own life. Augustine impresses modern people as too severe. To the Pelagians he was too lax.

41.   Augustine will continue using various of the organizational categories already employed—the five senses, for instance, or the four excitements of the soul. But now he places these within a threefold scheme given him by the text of John's First Letter (2.16): "For the things of this world are the urges of the flesh, the urges of the eyes, and worldly designs." In his *Interpreting John's Parthian Letter*, he says these are "things of the world" only in the sense that they represent the general traits of sinful mankind in the world. The created world of God is good in itself. Only when worldly goods are considered in themselves, as apart from God, do they become sinful. He uses this striking comparison:

> Say a fiancé has a ring made for his bride-to-be. If, when she takes it, she falls more in love with the ring than with him, does

she not commit a kind of adultery with the ring? . . . He has given you a pledge to bring you closer to him, not to push you off from him. The pledge was given so that he would be loved in it. In this way God has given you everything. Love him who gave it. He wants to give you even more—in fact, to give you himself, the maker of all that he gives. But if you love all these things, which God has admittedly given, but neglect the giver who created them, to concentrate your love on the world, do you not commit adultery with the world? (2.11)

Augustine's interpretation of the Latin text of 1 John 2.16 is far enough from the Greek original (obscure in itself) and from modern translations of the Greek that the difference should be noted here. A literal translation of the Greek is: "Everything in the world—the desire of [or for] the flesh, the desire of [or for] the eyes, and the grandiosity [*alazoneia*] of life—is not from the Father." Attempts to make sense of this lead to translations as different as these:

NEW ENGLISH BIBLE: "Everything the world affords, all that panders to the appetites or entices the eyes, all the glamour of its life, springs not from the Father." (This version takes the first two genitives as objective—desire as an enticement *to* the flesh and to the eyes.)

ANCHOR BIBLE (RAYMOND BROWN): "For all that is in the world— human nature full of desire, eyes hungry for all they see, material life that inflates self-assurance—does not belong to the Father." (Brown takes the genitives as subjective—the flesh's own desire, the eyes' own desire.)

Augustine, like Brown, takes the genitives as subjective, though he gives a special meaning to "eyes." But instead of *alazoneia* (grandiosity) and *biou* (life) for the third item, the Latin form used in Africa gave Augustine *ambitio* (encompassment) and *saeculi* (the age, or time, or world). What are we to make of these?

We might have expected Augustine to use a more conventional set of norms by which to measure his spiritual life—the Ten Commandments, perhaps, or the seven deadly sins, or the vices opposed to the theological and natural virtues. But at the time when he wrote *The Testimony*, he considered this Johannine text the most comprehensive catalogue of moral failures, probably because it was a *triple* formula. He used it subtly throughout earlier books of *The Testimony*, in ways carefully traced by O'Donnell—see his index citing all uses of the passage (3.477). Augustine connected the passage with three distortions of the Trinity in man, with Jesus' three trials in the desert, and with three heraldic animal symbols of vice. A panel of these parallels would look like this:

Urges	Trinity	Jesus (Trials)	Animals
Flesh's urges	Spirit of love	Fleshly love (change bread)	Sheep
Eyes' urges	Word's wisdom	Magic (hurl self down)	Serpent
Worldly designs	Father's grandeur	Worldly power	Bird

To see how he built on this schematic approach, we should take each of the three items separately.

1. *The flesh's urges*. In his book on John's First Letter, Augustine says these urges have to do with all the wants of the body—

mainly food, drink, and sex. The animal nutrition suggests a sheep, and the bread that Jesus is asked to provide from a stone, and the wants of the Holy Spirit. In order to examine himself in this area, he will go through the sequence of senses again (for the fourteenth time), testing whether he is imprisoned by any of the five or has attained some degree of mastery over them.

2. *The eyes' urges.* Since he has already considered the eyes' physical wants under the sense of sight, he finds that the eyes here stand for what the *mind* "sees"—that is, for knowledge. What could be an illicit urge here? He lists the kinds of *transgressive* knowledge he has in mind by the term *curiositas*— "the pagan games of the circus and theater, diabolic rites, magical arts, and evil spells" (*Interpreting John's First Letter* 2.13). Though these were real temptations to others, it is hard to think he was seriously tempted by any of them. So he is reduced to saying that wanting God to answer prayer automatically is a kind of magic, and he must not want prayer to "work" but only to accommodate him to what God decrees.

3. *Worldly designs.* Ambitio means, literally, encompassment, "going around" (*amb-ire*). It was used of politicians "going around" seeking votes. Then it was used of any "roundabout" means of soliciting support—for power or fame or glory. Augustine has the etymology very much in mind when he says of himself: "Every word pronounced, every act performed, before others incurs the dangerous test of wooing praise, wheedling a coaxed [*emendicata*] endorsement of one's self-estimate" **[63]**. *Emendicata* is an electioneering term. For him, the temptation was not to worldly power but to praise and

renown. I use "worldly designs" to cover the whole matter of maneuvering (going about) for self-aggrandizement. As we shall see, Augustine does not think in terms of worldly power but of worldly renown as his special temptation under this heading of "worldly designs."

1. The Five Senses: Touch

It seems unrealistic to us for a celibate man not yet forty years old to think of being free from night imaginings in conjunction with seminal emission. We must not think that Augustine considered these sinful. If that were so, he says, then a woman's periodic menstruation would have to be considered sinful (*What Good There Is in Marriage* 20). He admits that both acts were considered "impurities" under Jewish ritual law, but he says that was a symbolic matter that has been abrogated by the New Testament (ibid.). In this paragraph he is interested in the integrity of the person, and how that has been lost by original sin. That is: *granting* that it is not sinful to have such imaginations in one's dreams, *why* is it not? Because there are two persons, one responsible and one not? But if that is the case, then why can he sometimes resist the lustful images even in his sleep? In that case, any bright-line boundary between his sleeping and his waking self seems blurred. Does he really have two selves? And can they sometimes invade each other's territory? The drama of Jekyll and Hyde is adumbrated here—and the whole issue of a subconscious (or at least of a subresponsible conscious). Can there be an integration of the two selves in this life?

42.   Augustine says that the subconscious self could be freed from sexual hauntings, but only by God's grace. Why even consider this? Because it was a boast of the desert ascetics that they had so starved and beaten their bodies that they were now exempt from sexual fantasies (see Peter Brown, *The Body and Society*, pp. 230–32, 422–23). Augustine is saying that even they did not "earn" the exemption, since only grace can achieve it, and that is freely given. In their case, perhaps, the grace was the gift that enabled them to undergo the heroic mortifications in the first place. But Augustine is admitting to his flock that he has not reached that level of grace. Their bishop is as vulnerable to sexual dreams as any of them. It is daylight resistance that matters.

2. The Five Senses: Taste

45.   Augustine, unlike his mother (T 9.17–18), had no problem with alcohol. (He tells us at [13] that he naturally prefers honey to wine.) He sees, though, that there is a temptation for him in this area: to take pride in his own sobriety. He has to keep reminding himself that this is God's gift to him—as is the grace given others (like his mother) to be cured of insobriety.

46.   Augustine uses Paul's dispute over the kosher laws to oppose the purists of his own day, the Manichaeans, who forbade their "perfect" from eating meat. Pride in diet, Augustine believes, is more sinful than modest eating of whatever sort. To show that what one eats is not the norm by which one should be judged, he lists seven "eating texts" from the Bible, involving:

1. Noah (Genesis 9.2): meat
2 Elijah (1 Kings 17.6): meat
3. The Baptist (Matthew 3.4): locusts
4. Esau (Genesis 25.34): lentils
5. David (2 Samuel 23.15 ff.): water
6. Jesus (Matthew 4.3): bread
7. The people in Exodus (Numbers 11.1 ff.): manna

3. The Five Senses: Smell

48. This paragraph is perfunctory, since Augustine has no particular temptation with regard to perfume. But once he has accepted the category of the senses for his self-examination, he must be inclusive. Otherwise it might be thought he was omitting something to hide something. The pilot must go through every item on his checklist before takeoff.

4. The Five Senses: Hearing

49.–50. Music did pose difficulties for Augustine. His scruples may seem fussy to us, but his position was delicate, as was that of his church. The rival Donatist communities were known for their raucous singing. Sometimes Augustine was glad to have the sound of his community singing late into the night outlast the Donatist church that was within hearing distance of his cathedral (Letter 29.11). But he, like Ambrose from whom he learned the use of church music, had to restrain the kind of exuberance that burst out into dancing and wild behavior. The use of antiphonal chanting was an innovation in Africa during

the 390s. Some of the popular new singing was as much resisted as modern singing in the liturgies of our time. A few of
the songs became popular hits. The opening verse of Psalm 132
was so beloved that Augustine said: "Even those who do not
know [anything else from] the Psalms sing that sweet melody.
It is as sweet as the charity that unites brothers in harmony"
(*Explaining the Psalms* 132.1).

A hasty first reading of **[49–50]** might give the impression
that Augustine was a puritan about music. That was far from
the case. He recommended that his monks sing to cheer themselves at work (*The Office of Monks* 17.20). When his mother
rebuked one of his pupils for singing a hymn while using the
outhouse, and the boy kidded her ("Do you think if an enemy
locked me in there, God would not hear me call for help?"), Augustine took the boy's side (*Order in the Universe* 1.8). In a
sermon of his book *Explaining the Psalms* (66.6) he said:

> Travelers seek to ease the burden of the way. So sing you along
> the way. I urge you in the name of our Way, sing along the way,
> sing a new song, none of the old, sing a patriotic song of your
> homeland [heaven]. No more old songs. New is the way, new
> the traveler, and new the song. . . . Travelers sing, especially at
> night, when scary things make omninoises [*circumstrepunt*]—
> or, rather, omnisilences [*circumsilent*], the scarier the omni-
> silenter. Those also sing who fear robbers. How much safer
> your song in Christ—this Way has no robbers along it, unless
> you fall in with one by leaving the Way. . . . Your song is your
> testimony [*confessio*].

In one of Augustine's later-discovered sermons (Dolbeau 198.11), he exhorts his congregation to vociferous song:

> Fraternal unison lends ardor to our prayer and praise of God—as when a ponderous mass has to be transported, and a song is raised to the heave-ho rhythm; would not the sheer number of voices united in shouting and straining, united even more in the oneness of the effort, infect even your fainting hearts and make you want to tug at the ropes for sheer joy of the task to be done? That is the way shared feeling strengthens our love.

Normally Augustine demands that the words of scripture not be drowned by the melody. But he expressed delight in exuberant Hallelujahs, and in one revealing passage he admits that emotion can rightly outrun clarity of reasoning:

> When men sing in the fields or the vineyards or at other sweaty work, and express their cheerfulness in the words of a song, they can be so filled with cheer that the words no longer express it, and they give up on the words to make mere sounds of gladness. These sounds show that their hearts are more full than any words can say. Well, who better deserves such sounds of gladness than the inexpressible God? He is inexpressible since you cannot express what he is. And if you are not able to express that, and are not allowed to be silent, what else is there but to make glad noises, showing your heart's wordless joy, an unconfined joy not to be measured out in syllables? (*Explaining the Psalms* 32, second sermon 8)

He led into that passage by telling his congregation that everyone should sing, even if they cannot keep tune or time, since the heart's love is being expressed, not an artist's perfectionism. It is the repeated Augustinian message: Song is not at fault, but pride in song is.

5. The Five Senses: Sight

52.   As Augustine listed scriptural passages having to do with food [46], he now lists examples of spiritual light. Throughout this section Augustine is not trying to deny or renounce the physical senses, but to subordinate them to the spiritual senses, of which they are a sign or a means of access.

1. *Tobias* (*Tobias* 4.1–23): The blind Tobias blesses his son, saying (among other things): "At all times bless the Lord and ask that he direct your path" (4.20). Augustine's comments on this passage at *Interpreting John's Gospel* 13.3: "Tobias was not deprived of eyesight when, though physically blind, he gave his son the counsels of life. The son took his father's hand to guide his steps while the father showed him the way to tread the path to justice."

2. *Isaac* (*Genesis* 27.1–40): Isaac is deceived when he tries to bless Esau, but God means for Jacob to be blessed. God writes straight with crooked lines.

3. *Jacob* (*Genesis* 48.17–22). Again, a son tries to steer his father wrong, but the inner vision foresees a blessed line of descendents. The figure involved in "rays from his heart" comes from the fact that Augustine, like most of his contemporaries, thought that the human eye emitted rays in the act of vision.

Though Jacob's eyes can no longer do that, God's light emits rays *from his heart.*

In "lay claim to the light by singing of you," Augustine describes how one keeps the spiritual light alive by praise of God even when physical light goes away during the night. We saw earlier (**[49–50]** *comm.*) how men sing at night to keep away robbers. Now he says that a singing in the soul keeps one awake to the Lord rather than wrapped up in one's own night dreams. Singing to keep awake was a commonplace in ancient literature (see Aeschylus, *Agamemnon* 17; Aristophanes, *Clouds* 720–21, Lucretius, *The Way Things Are* 1405). Ambrose introduced song to keep his Milan congregation vigilant when it occupied his church, day and night, against the attempts of the Empress Justina to seize it (T 9.15). In the penumbra of this sentence, notice the quickly following, "*You sleep not, nor slumber. . . .*"

53.   All the wonders of human creativity are only an "entrapment" if they are considered apart from the God who makes them possible—first by giving an artist the materials he can refashion, and second by giving him the inner light by which to refashion them creatively. Admiring the beauties of vision apart from God is a form of idolatry—in the same way that it is a form of infidelity to worship the engagement ring rather than the fiancé who gave it **[41]** *comm.* Artists who "worship" things made by their own hand are really worshiping themselves rather than the God who gave them their talent.

V. Transgressive Knowledge (*curiositas*)

54. *Curiositas* is not "curiosity" in our sense. Any mere trivialization of sight fits under the preceding treatment of the sense of vision [51–52]. "To see" in this place means "to know." And the knowledge condemned is one that tries to surpass the legitimate boundaries of the knowable, moving in two principal directions—the perverse (sadomasochistic) and the occult (sacrilegious).

55. He begins with a masochistic example—necrophilia, the deliberate cultivation of painful sensations in viewing a corpse. This shows the serious nature of *curiositas* in the technical sense Augustine is giving that term. It is a perverse desire to "know everything," to have a kind of godlike indifference to everything except the drive to break boundaries and see the forbidden. This is the bargain with the devil that is condemned in Faust or Dr. Frankenstein, but especially in Eve as she tastes of the tree of knowledge. The second category is knowledge of the occult, all the uses of magic to make knowledge "work," to press springs in the hidden mechanism of the universe.

57. How can gossip be fit into Augustine's criticism of transgressive knowledge? It does not seem to belong to either of the two categories brought up so far—sadomasochism or occultism. Gossip is not condemned simply because it wastes time. Augustine is willing to waste some time in humoring another. He turns censorious when he becomes interested in the gossip itself. His problem with that is indicated in the doggerel he carved into the monastery table at Hippo (Possidius, *Life of Saint Augustine* 21):

> Who gnaws with gossip [*dictis*] those who are away
> May not bite food or at this table stay.

So there is a sadistic temptation in gossip, the Schadenfreude that is its staple.

What about the other small test he mentions—watching a hound course a hare? The clue here is his introductory reference to the circus. His condemnation of the cruel displays in the Roman arena was directed against Alypius's addiction to "the games' insanity" (T 6.11). Augustine himself had in his earlier days been a fan of cockfights (*Order in the Universe* 1.25). The animal fight in the field no doubt reminded him of these pagan pleasures, as does even the trapping of insects. These are admittedly slight cases of "blood lust," but blood lust was not a slight thing to one familiar with the cruel pagan spectacles.

VI. Worldly Designs

59. For this category see *comm.* at **[41]**. Clearly Augustine, with great self-knowledge, sees this as his major failing, the desire for praise and renown. He is most thorough in his self-questioning here, where he admits that it is most difficult. When I wrote a brief biography of Augustine, and said that he posted the penitential psalms around his deathbed to pray for forgiveness of his sins, an editor told me that I should put in a vivid flashback to his days of sexual indulgence, as if that were the only sin he could have in mind. But he did not have to go back nearly half a century to find the roots of his self-centeredness.

60. Where other weaknesses are concerned, Augustine can measure their extent or intensity by experiment upon himself. He can test the effect of depriving himself of sex or money, to see how attached to them he has become. But he cannot forbid others to praise him. That would stifle a generous impulse in them and probably just lead to a greater pride in him for rising above their praise—see **[64]**. Praise goes with a good life, and he cannot give up the good life to see whether he can give up praise. He tries to make up for this lack of experimental examination of himself by a series of thought experiments.

61. First experiment: Can he prefer denigration for good conduct to praise for bad conduct? He is confident that he can. But he cannot say that he is indifferent to the denigration, even so, or that he would not like to have the praise that is denied him by good conduct. And when he finds these weaknesses in himself, he searches for excuses, a giveaway that they *are* indeed weaknesses.

Second experiment: This looks beyond simple pleasure in praise or dislike of criticism to see if he ranks others' comments, either praising or critical, according to whether they correspond with his own self-estimate. To his dismay, he finds that he does rank them this way, which proves he is not looking primarily to the benefit of others but to his amour propre.

62. Third experiment: He asks himself if he resents false accusations directed against others less than those directed at himself, even if the accusations are equally false. Again he has to admit that he is not looking simply to the justice of each situation. He makes his own case special.

63. Fourth experiment: If he tries to avoid coaxing praise from others, he takes pride in that forbearance, showing he does not escape the need for praise after all.

64. Fifth experiment: Could he break entirely his dependence on others' praise without falling into the worst of all pits, self-praise, the supreme arrogance of Satan? He has to

admit that he could not. All he can do is throw himself on the mercy of God and hope for grace to do by God's power what he cannot do himself. Pelagius, who derided this reliance on grace, was an example of the pride involved in virtue conscious of itself.

VII. Conclusion

65.–70.   Concluding his self-examination, he sees no escape from his own weakness except by the intervention of a mediator who takes on human weakness to redeem it with divine strength. That mediator alone can carry him on to a search for the Trinity in Scripture, the one task left to Augustine in *The Testimony*.

PART IV

Appendix: *The Testimony,* Book Eleven

I. Prayer Before Studying Scripture

1.   Surely, Lord, you cannot be ignorant of anything I tell you, nor in your eternity do you see time simply as it develops. Then why do I arrange in sequence what I narrate for you? I do it, not as informing you, but as stirring up my own reaction to you, and so that people reading this may say 'vast is the Lord, and as vast should be his praise.' As I have maintained, and still maintain, this is done out of love for your love. We continue to pray, even though Truth itself tells us 'Your father knows what you need before you ask him for it.' We lay open to you our reaction to you, testifying to our pitiable state and your pity for it, so you may free us entirely as you have already partly done, making us no longer pitiful in ourselves but happy in you, since you have called us to be 'poor in spirit, gentle, mournful, hungry and thirsty for justice, merciful, pure in heart, and bringers of peace.'

That is why I have offered you this long account, to the best of my ability and desire, since 'your goodness shows in your endless pity.'   2.   And now I have the opportunity for 'my pen to articulate' the whole of your encouragements, your warnings and consolings and guidings, by which you brought me to preach your word and share your mysteries with your people. Even if I have the opportunity, still, to continue my narrative, the water drops of time are too precious for me to do so—I have for too long been 'burning with a need to study your law,' to testify about what it is I understand and what I have no sense of—through the dawning of your light and the lingering shades of my own night—and how far my frailty has been taken up into your strength. I would not have any hours diverted from this, apart from those I must spend on the restoration of the body, the drawing together of the mind's resources, and the services I owe, or pay without owing, to others.

3. 'Hear my prayer,' Lord my God, let your pity assist my desire, aflame not only for my own enlightenment but for service to my brothers in love. You know this of me, since you see my heart. For me to offer up my thought and voice to your service, grant me what I may offer. Of myself 'I am without resource and poor,' but you prove 'wealthy for all who call on you.' Free of care, you care for us. 'Circumcise my lips' from every rash or deceptive utterance, outward or within me. Purify my delight in your scripture, so I am neither misled in them myself nor misleading others. Lord, draw near, Lord my God, and pity, you light of the blind and strength for the frail—and light, as well, for the seeing, strength for the vigorous. Draw near my soul and hear me 'crying from the abyss.' If you do not hear in the abyss, what resource have we? To whom shall we cry?

Yours are the days, the nights, the moments that flit by as you decree. Lengthen my days for the study of your law's inner meanings. Open the door to them when I knock on it.

You had a purpose in causing the scripture to contain so many pages dark with obscure meaning. This dense wood shelters deer who have taken refuge in it, restoring their strength, pacing its lanes and grazing there, resting and ruminating. Lord, make me complete for the receiving of these matters. I take my joy in what you say, richer than piled-up pleasures. Grant what I love, for the fact that I love was itself your grant. Leave me not, keep what you planted from withering. May I testify to whatever I find in your books, and hear 'the voice of your praise,' and drink from you, and 'ponder the marvels of your law' all the way back to the origin of what you made, heaven and earth, all the way forward to the perpetual reign to be shared with you in the city you make holy.

4. Let your pity, Lord, assist my desire—it is not, I believe, a desire for worldly things, for gold or silver or gems or fine vestures, honors or power or sensual pleasures. Nor is it for the requirements of the body as we pass through this pilgrimage of life—all these will be 'supplied to those in quest of your reign and justice.' You behold, my God, the source of my yearning. 'The wicked have described their delights, but they are nothing to your law, O Lord.' Behold the source of my yearning. Behold it, Father, and seeing it, prosper it. Favoring me with your pitying gaze, open as I knock the way to your words' inmost meaning. I ask this of you through our Lord Jesus Christ, 'the man of your right arm, the son of man, whom you have appointed as your mediator with us.' Through him you sought us out who were not seeking you, and sought us in order that we might seek you. He is your word, through whom

you created all things, and me among them. He is your only-begotten, through whom you have called the company of believers, and among them me, into your sonship. I ask you through him 'who sits at your right hand and interposes himself on our behalf.' 'In him are all the hidden treasures of wisdom and of knowledge.' These are what I seek in your books. Moses wrote of him, who speaks here himself—the truth speaks to us.

II. Genesis on Creation

5. May I listen so as to grasp how 'in the origin you made heaven and earth.' Moses wrote these words, wrote them and departed from us, passing from us to you, and he is not here in my sight. If he were, I would clasp him to me and would request, would beg through you, for him to explain these words to me, I would bring my ears up close to every word flowing from his mouth,—not that I could understand him if he spoke Hebrew, which would knock at my ears without reaching inward to my intellect. But if he could speak Latin, I would know what he was saying. Yet even then how could I know that what he was saying was true? If I did know that, it would not be on his word that I relied. Within me, where my thoughts are at home, truth itself would speak, not in Hebrew or Greek or Latin, or any uncouth tongue, it would speak without the body's organs, without mouth or tongue, without the sounding out of syllables. It would tell me that Moses spoke true, and I would confidently assent to your emissary, admitting that he spoke true. Since, in any event, I cannot cross-examine him, you are the one I beg, you who inspired him to speak true, you the truth itself, you I ask for forgiveness of my sins, and ask that you make me understand the truths that you made him utter.

6. Look at heaven and earth. They proclaim that they were created by the fact that they change and do not remain the same. A thing that exists without being created has nothing missing from it that it ever was. That would be evidence of change—it is not all that it once was. They proclaim, as well, that they did not create themselves—that they had to be created, and that they could not pre-exist themselves to create themselves. They proclaim this by the very way they exist. For they are beautiful (since you are beautiful who made them), and good (because you are good), and existing (because you do)—but they do not have the beauty or goodness or being of you, their creator. Their beauty and goodness and being are as nothing compared with yours—as our knowledge of this fact (which is from you) is as nothing compared with your knowledge.

7. How did you make heaven and earth? What apparatus of construction had you for so huge a project? You did not work like a human artisan reshaping physical materials to give them the form seen within by the directing mind. Where could that directing mind come from but you? But for all the soul's directing power, it gives form only to things already in existence and having some prior form, whether as clay or stone or wood or gold or whatever. And these would not have existence already if you had not contrived it. You are the creator of the artist's body, of the soul that works its limbs, of the material he reshapes, of the talent that masters his art and devises internally what he will fashion externally, of the body's perceptual sys-

tem that transmits his design from the mind into the stuff he works, and then reports back to the mind what was made, so it can compare it with the inner model to see if it corresponds with it. All these things praise all things' creator.

How did you bring all these things about? In the way you created heaven and earth—because you did not make heaven or earth out of their own materials, not out of air or water (for they are just elements of heaven and earth). The whole cosmos could not be made out of the whole cosmos, since no place existed for making it until it was made to exist. You had no manual tool for manufacturing heaven and earth. For where would you get a tool for creation that you had not already created? What exists but from your existence? You used your Word to make them, and in your Word they were made.

8. How was that Word spoken? Not as the voice came from a cloud to say 'This is the son I love.' That voice sounded and ceased, it had a beginning and end. The syllables were enunciated and passed by, the second after the first, third after the second, each succeeding in its time, and silence succeeded the last. It is evident from this that the voice was caused by changes in the physical surroundings—serving your timeless purpose, it is true, but temporal in themselves. These words sounding in time were passed through the ear to the judicious mind, whose interior ear is alert to your timeless word. The mind compared the words sounding in time against the timeless word heard in silence, and concluded that they were entirely different things. The sounding words are a lesser thing

than man, in fact are nothing at all, since they flew by and are gone. The Word of God, however, is a greater thing than man, since it changes never.

If, in order to make heaven and earth, you had said 'Let there be heaven and earth' in sounding and passing words, there would have been a physical medium before the creation of heaven and earth, a medium in which the words could make changes in time in order to run though their temporal sequence. But no physical stuff existed before heaven and earth. And even if it had, you would not have made it with a passing voice, since what was being made would be the medium for the passing voice in which it would be said, 'Let there be heaven and earth.' And whatever was the stuff of which that voice should be fashioned, it would not have existed unless you made it. So what word did you use to make the physical stuff of which the words could be made?

9.   You summon us, then, to understand 'the Word that is God in company with God,' which is eternally uttered and in which all things are eternally uttered. In it one thing is not said so that another may succeed it, with others to follow to the end, but all is said at once and for all time. Were this not so, time and change would already exist, not eternity and immortality. This much at least I know, my God, and I thank you for the knowledge, testify to my knowledge before you, and anyone knows it along with me who blesses you, who resists not your unshakable truth. We know this, Lord, know it for a certainty: insofar as anything is not now what it was before, or was before what it

is not now, it is a thing that dies or comes into being. But your Word does not fade out or follow in sequence, it is immortal and eternal. Therefore it is with a Word that is eternal that you utter, all at once and for all time, all things you utter, and whatever you utter comes to be. And it comes to be by nothing *but* your utterance. But what you utter is not, like the utterance itself, all at once and for all time.

10.   Why should this be so, I ask you, Lord my God? I have some grasp of it, but how to explain it is beyond me, unless I can put it this way: All things that begin to be or cease being do so when your eternal reason, which neither begins nor ceases, knows that it ought to begin or cease. That reason is your Word, 'the origin, since he speaks to us as such'—for so in the gospel [of John] he spoke in his incarnate self, and these words sounded externally in men's ears, that it might be believed and internally examined, and understood in the eternal truth where all learn from him who is the true and 'only teacher.'

There I listen to your voice speaking to me—for all teachers must speak to us, and those not teaching might speak without speaking to us—and who can teach but the immutable truth? Even when we are pointed toward the truth by a mutable human, we are being guided toward the immutable truth where we truly learn by waiting for and listening to him and, overjoyed with 'joy at the Bridegroom's voice,' we return ourselves to our own origin. He is our origin, since we would have no place to return after wandering unless he were continuously there. And whenever we return from wandering, it is by understanding that we are returning, and he teaches us to understand this because he is 'the origin insofar as he speaks to us.'

11.   It was at the origin that you made heaven and earth, God, in your Word, your Son, your power and wisdom and truth, by wondrous utterance and wondrous creation. Who can take it in? Who can give an account of it? What is this light that shines through me and transfixes my heart without cutting it? I shudder off from it and burn toward it, shuddering off because I am so deeply unlike it, burning toward because I am so deeply like it. It is Wisdom, personified Wisdom that shines through me, piercing the shades that so obnubilate me that I faint under the light, from my own darkness and the burden of my punishments. 'My energy is drained by my own neediness,' and I cannot sustain my own well-being until you 'look kindly on all my evil inclinations and treat all their symptoms.' For you will buy my life back from its decay, and honor me with your compassion and pity, and so fulfill my yearnings with good things that 'my youth will come back to me as an eagle's.' It is 'hope that rescues us,' and we await with confidence what you have promised. Let anyone who can do so, heed you speaking inwardly, but I will outwardly speak with confidence from your own revealed words: 'How wondrous are your works, Lord, all that you have in your wisdom created!' That wisdom is the origin in which he created heaven and earth.

12.   What but 'old nature, unredeemed' makes people ask what God was doing before he made heaven and earth? If, they say, he was at leisure and did not busy himself, why did he not

stay that way indefinitely, continuing to refrain from labor as he had in the past? If something new occurred to God as the result of a new decision on his part, to create something he had never done before, how could there be a genuine eternity where a decision not formerly made was eventually made? That decision is not itself a creature, but has to be made before the creation, since nothing would be made if no decision to make it had been formed. So the decision had to be part of God's very being—and if part of his very being occurs that was not there before, his being cannot be called eternal. If, on the other hand, the decision to create was eternal, then why is not the resulting creation eternal?

13.   Those who argue that way have not even begun—no, God of wisdom, Light of minds, they have not begun—to see how things are made in you and by you. They try to savor everlasting things, but their heart flits back and forth between things that have passed and are still to come, and remain sterile. Who will catch and calm the heart, so a gradual stillness will come over it, and a gradual gaining on eternal quiet, to be compared with the unquietness of time, and to be found incompatible with it? Then it can see that a time is made long only by a succession of many things moving past. If they all occurred at the same time, it would not be a long time. In eternity there is no such succession of things, the entirety is present, and that cannot be a time. In time, the past is shoved away by the arriving future, and the future trails behind the past, and both past and future are constituted by the present they flow through. Who will catch and calm the heart, to see in stillness how it is

the stillness of eternity that controls past and future, without itself being either past or future? Is my hand up to this great work, can the words from my mouth catch and calm like a hand?

14. How do I respond to those who ask what God was doing before he made heaven and earth? Not as one is said to have responded by way of jest, to avoid the brunt of the question, claiming God spent the time getting hell ready for those who pry into serious matters. Since mocking is not solving, I would not say that. Rather than have one person mocked for asking a serious question and another person flattered for answering with a smart lie, I would, if I did not know the true answer, simply say I do not know. But I say that you, our God, are the creator of all creatures; and since all creation is included in the term heaven and earth, I can answer boldly that 'at the time' before he made heaven and earth he was *not*, in fact, doing anything—if he had been, it would have been making heaven and earth; and I wish I were as sure of other things it would profit me to know as I am that no created thing was created before creation.

15. But if someone of unsteady mind, shuffling representations of times past, is astonished that you, the omnipotent, the omni-creant, the omni-tenant, should have waited through numberless ages before making such an imposing world, he will see that his astonishment is misplaced if he just rouses himself and pays heed. How could there have been numberless ages before you made them, you who make and begin all things? What times could have been before you began them?

How could times pass before they were there for the passing? Since you set all times in motion, if there were any times before you made heaven and earth, how could anyone say you were doing nothing 'at the time'? You would have been creating time, and there could be no time past until you made time first. If there was no time before heaven and earth, you could not have been doing anything then—since there was no time, there was no *then*.

16.   There is with you no time before time—if so, you would not be before that time; yet you are before all times. In your transcendent present state of eternity, you are before all past time and after all future time, since the future is still to come and when it comes it will be the past, but you are ever the same, and 'your years wither not.' Your years neither come nor go; but ours do come and go, so that all may file by. Your years stand all together, since they move not, and departing years cannot be driven out by arriving ones, since none recede. Our years will not be entire until they are entirely gone, but your years are one day, not one in a series but a today that yields to no tomorrow and follows on no yesterday. Eternity is your today, so you eternally beget the Son to whom you said, 'Today I have begotten you.' All times are made by you, who are before them. There was never a *time* when time was not.

17.   There was, therefore, no time before you made anything, since time itself is something you made. No time could be eternal along with you, since you are always there; and if time were always, it would not be time. Then what is time? Who can give that a brief or easy answer? Who can even form a

conception of it to be put in words? Yet what do we mention more often or familiarly in our conversation than time? We must therefore know what we are talking about when we refer to it, or when we hear someone else doing so. But what, exactly, is that? I know what it is if no one asks; but if anyone does, then I cannot explain it. But this at least I can venture: If nothing were passing away, there would be no past time; and if nothing were still coming, there would be no future time; and if nothing were passing, there would be no present time. But what mode of existence can those first two times have, since the past is no longer and the future is not yet? And the third time, the present, if it were not passing away, would not be the present but the eternal. But if the present is only a time because it is passing away, how we can say that it exists, since the reason for its existing *as time* is that it will soon not be, which means we can only say it exists because it is on its way to non-existence?

18.   Yet we speak of time as being long or short, though it is only about the past or future that we say this. We say a long time from now, in the past, when we mean a century or so ago, or in the future when we mean a century or so hence. A short time means, say, ten days ago (for the past) or ten days hence (for the future). But how can something that has no being be long or short? The past no longer is, the future is not yet. So perhaps we should not say a time is long but that it was long, or will be long. Lord, my illumination, is your truth just having fun with man? Does a long time past become long when it has passed away, or was it long while it was passing in the present? It could only be long when what was being long *was*. When it

had passed away it no longer *was*, so it could not *be* long. So we should not say that something was a long time ago, since we cannot establish what was long if we try to find it in a past that is no more. Should we, rather, say that it *was* a long *present* time, since its passing through the present was long? Before it had passed away, there was some being that could be long; but as soon as it passed away, it ceased to be long because it ceased to be.

19.   I ask you, my human mind, since you experience the lapses of time and their measurement, whether present time can be long. Come, what is your answer? The current century, is that a long time? First we must ask how a whole century could be in the present. Take year one of the century. If we are in it, then we still have ninety-nine years to go, and we are not yet in those, since they are still in the future. If we are in the second year, then one year is in the past and the rest are in the future. And so with any year down the line, whenever it is present, the rest will be either in the past or in the future. So the century as a whole cannot be in the present. What about the year we are in, can that at least be present to us? But here, too, if we are in the first month, the rest are to come. If in the second, the first is gone and the rest are still coming. So the present year is not present as a whole, and if not present as a whole then not present as a year. There are, after all, twelve months in a year, and if any of the twelve is present, the other eleven are either in the future or in the past. But not even one of these months is actually present, but only one day at a time—if the first, then the rest are to come; if the last, then the

rest are already gone; and if any day between, the rest are divided between past and future.

20.   See, now, how the present time, which we saw as the only one that can be called long, has been reduced to barely a day—no, we have to amend that, since not even a day can be present. A day is nighttime and daytime, twenty-four hours, and the first hour leaves the rest still to come, the last leaves the rest behind it, and any other stands between past and future. And each hour is itself articulated into fleeting minutes. Those that have already flown off are in the past, and the rest are still in the future. If we suppose some particle of time which could not be divided into a smaller particle, that alone deserves to be called the present. Yet it flies in so headlong a way out of the future and into the past that no slightest moment of rest can reach itself out in pause. If it paused, its earlier part could be divided from its later. Thus the present itself has no length.

Then is there any time we can call long? How about future time? Well, we cannot say that *is* a long time since there is not yet anything to be long—we have to say it *will be* a long time. When? Not while it is still in the future, since it must first be in order to be long. But when it moves out of the future, which is not yet, into the present, where it can *be*, and therefore be *long*, the present vociferates what we have already heard, that the present cannot be long, either.

21.   For all that, Lord, we observe the different ways times lapse, and compare them, and call some longer and some shorter. In fact, we measure how much longer or shorter one time is than another, and we conclude that one is twice or thrice

as long as another, or perhaps of the same length. It is passing time we measure, as we experience it. For who can measure past time, which is no more, or future time, which is not yet, unless he is bold enough to claim that he can measure non-being. So time can only be measured as it passes. Once past, it is no longer there to be measured.

22. These are queries, Father, not conclusions. Control and guide me, my God. Will anyone claim that what we learned as children and teach our children is not true after all, that there are *not* three tenses, past, present, and future, but only the present, and that the other two do not exist? Or that the other two exist, but only as something emerging out of mystery, when the future turns into the present, and merging into mystery, when the present turns into the past? If, after all, the future did not exist, how could prophets foretell it? There would be nothing there to foretell. And if the past does not exist, how could historians uses their minds to put together a true account of it? There would be nothing to put together.

23. Help me, you ground of my hope, to deepen my queries. Steady my searching mind. If the future and the past are, I wish to know where they are. If I cannot learn that, I can at least be sure that wherever they are, they are not there as the future or the present, but both are the present. For if the future is there as the future, it is not there yet. And if the past is there as the past, it is no longer there. So whatever they are, and wherever there, they must be there in the present. When a history of the past is truly related, the memory does not bring back the events themselves, which have gone out of existence,

but the words describing them—and these words were taken from the senses as the events left on them a print of their passage. My boyhood, for example, which no longer exists, is in the past, which also no longer exists. Then what does? A representation of it does—that is what I see in the present, stored in my memory, whenever I remember or recount my boyhood. Does something similar happen in prophecy, representations of what does not yet exist being somehow made present in the mind of the prophet? I cannot tell that, my God, but at least I know this, that we often make provisions for our future actions, and the provisions exist, because they are in the present, but the actions do not exist, because they are still in the future. But when we come to perform the actions for which we made provisions, then the actions will exist, since they are no longer future, but present.

24. Whatever occurs when secrets of the future are foreseen, they could not be foreseen if they did not exist. And what exists is in the present, not the future. So when some are said to foretell the future, they are not seeing the future, which does not yet exist because it is still to come—perhaps they see some preconditions or indications of the future, which exist already. So to them the objects of their prediction are not future but present; they are materials from which the mind can form estimates of what will be. These estimates, too, are in the present, and those predicting the future are actually seeing their own present estimates.

From many possible examples of this, I cite one. Looking at the morning twilight, I predict the sun will rise. What I see is present, what I foresee is future—not that the sun will exist (it already does), but that its rise will exist. That has not yet occurred, so I could not predict its rise without having an image of that event in my mind (as I do even now when I mention it). Two things I see—the twilight preceding sunrise, which yet is not sunrise, and the image of sunrise in my mind, which is also not sunrise. Both these things must be seen in the present for the future to be predicted—the sun's rising. Future things are not yet. And if not yet, then not at all. And if they are not at all, they cannot be seen. But they can be predicted from things which already are, and are already seen.

25. What means do you employ, you ruler of the universe, for showing select souls the future—as you did the prophets? By what means do you, for whom there is no future, reveal the future? Or do you, rather, reveal present things that indicate the future? For what does not exist cannot be shown. Whatever means you use of showing the future is far, far beyond my range of vision. 'It unstrings me, I have no power.' But power I would have, sweet Light of my inmost eyes, if it were your gift.

26. What should be clear and obvious by now is that we cannot properly say that the future or the past exist, or that there are three times, past, present, and future. Perhaps we can say that there are three tenses, but that they are the present of the past, the present of the present, and the present of the future. This would correspond, in some sense, with a triad I find in the soul and nowhere else, where the past is present to memory, the present is present to observation, and the future is

present to anticipation. With this proviso, I can see and grant that there are three times after all; and the customary way of talking about three different times—past, present, and future—may be accepted, despite its imprecision. I do not worry, oppose, or criticize it, so long as one understands, beneath the language, that what is future is not yet, and that what is past is no longer. We rarely speak with real precision, but often use words loosely while understanding what is intended.

27. Earlier I said that we measure time as it passes, making us able to say that one time is twice as long as some other, or equal to it—and so of all other segments of time we can measure and describe. That is how we measure time as it passes. If someone should ask me how I know this, I answer that we are measuring something, that we cannot be measuring what does not exist, and that the past and future do not exist. But how can we measure the present, when it has no extent of its own? We must measure time as it passes, since it cannot be measured once it has passed, when it is no longer. Where does the time we are measuring come from, pass by, and pass to? Where from but the future? Where passing by but in the present? And where going but to the past? But that must mean that it comes from what does not exist yet, passes by what has no extent of its own, and goes to what exists no longer. Time must be measured in something with extent, or we could not say that things extend longer by double or triple or whatever amount. But in what extended thing do we measure time as it passes? In the future, from which time proceeds? We cannot

measure what is not yet. In the present, by which it proceeds? We cannot measure what has no extent. In the past, to which it proceeds? We cannot measure a thing that is no longer.

28. My mind has burned to understand this knotty problem. Do not seal, Lord my God and good Father, do not seal off from me things so esoteric yet so everyday, but open them to my longing and bathe them in the light of your pity for me. Is there anyone else I could learn from but you? What good would it do me to testify to my own ignorance before anyone but you? You are not annoyed by the importunacy of my burning need to know your scripture. Grant this thing I love, since my loving it was your grant. Grant it, Father, since you know how to make your gifts a boon to your children. Grant it, since I have set out on the path to understanding, and 'the task is beyond me' until you open a way for me. By Christ I beg you, for the honor of him who is the holy one of holies, let no one forbid my journey. 'I too have faith, from which I speak.' This is my ground of hope, for which I live, 'to contemplate the Lord's delights.' It is you who 'prolong my days into age,' yet their mode of passing is what I do not understand. We talk of this time and that, these times or those—of how long ago it was when this one spoke or that one acted. We say it has been a long time since we saw something, or that these syllables have twice the length of a single short one. That is how we talk, or hear others talk, and we are understood by others and understand them. It is the stuff of our everyday converse, yet it is all masked in darkness, and an understanding of it is still to be found.

29. A scholar once told me that time is nothing but the motion of the sun and moon and stars, without my agreeing. If that were true, why should not time be motion in any or all physical objects? If the lights of heaven should go out, but a potter's wheel were still turning, would there be no time by which we could measure its rotation, saying that each takes as long as the others? Or if some rotations are slower, others faster, can we not say that the former takes more time, the latter less? And in the act of saying this, do we not speak in time? Could we call syllables long or short unless some took a longer time, some a shorter time to pronounce? Grant to man, my God, to see in small matters principles that are common to small things and great. The stars and luminaries of the sky are there 'to serve as indications and times, as days and years.' I grant that, and would not maintain that a turn of the potter's wheel marks a day. But that scholar could not claim, either, that it does not mark a time.

30. I long to understand what time does and what it is, how we measure motion by it, and say, for example, that this motion takes twice the time of that one. This is my query: In the complete circuit of the sun around the earth, does the sun's motion itself constitute a day, or does the amount of time it takes, or both? We do not call a day simply the time when the sun is above the earth, marking day as distinct from night, but the whole time from one sunrise to the next, according to which we say so many days have passed, counting day and night together, with no separate status for night, but the entire circuit of the sun must be completed to make a day. If it is the

mere circuit that makes a day, then if the sun should speed around the earth in an hour, would that be a day? But if the amount of time consumed makes a day, then making the circuit in an hour would not constitute a day, but only the consumption of the full twenty-four hours. If it is *both* the circuit of the sun and the amount of time it takes that make a day, it could not be called a day if either of two things happened—if the sun made its circuit in an hour, or if it stopped in place for the twenty-four hours it normally takes to complete its circuit from sunrise to sunrise.

My query is not at this point about what we should call a day, but about the time we use for measuring the sun's motion—by which we might say that, if the sun made its circuit in twelve hours, it was taking only half the time it usually does. I am interested in the time we use when we compare the two and say that one is two times what the other is, no matter whether the sun goes from one sunrise to the next in the longer time or the shorter one. No one can tell me that time is the motion of celestial bodies, since there was a man at whose prayer the sun stood still, to carry a battle through to victory, and time kept going, though the sun did not. All the length of time that was needed to carry on and finish the battle was run through to completion. So I think that some kind of reach in opposite directions [toward future and past] is at issue here. I think that—or do I merely think I think it? You must settle the matter, my Light, my Truth.

31.   Do you require that I acquiesce when told that time is the motion of physical bodies? You do not. I hear that no body

moves except in time—you say it. I do not hear that the body's movement constitutes time—you do not say that. Time is what I use in order to measure the movement of a body, marking it from the beginning of the motion to its end—unless I fail to see the beginning and it continues on after I have stopped looking at it, and then I can only measure from the time I began looking to the point where I stopped. If I am watching for a long time, I can call that time long but I cannot tell *how* long the whole motion was, since we measure things by comparison, saying things like: This took the same time as that. Or: It was twice as long. And so on. But if we can pinpoint the expanses covered by the bodies, where the motion began and ended (or a turning began and ended, as on a lathe), we can say how long it took for the body to cover the distance marked out (or to make a complete turn). So the body's motion is one thing, and the way we measure how long that motion lasts is another—and who can doubt which of these should be called time? If a thing is sometimes moving and sometimes still, we can measure not only the motion but the still time, saying that it was still as long as it was moving, or it was still for twice or triple the time that it was moving, or whatever our estimate concludes or approximates (more or less, as we say). So time is not itself the motion of physical objects.

32. I testify to you, Lord, that I still do not know what time is; and testify as well, Lord, that I realize it takes time for me to say this—in fact, I have been speaking a long time about time, which could not have happened but by a lapse, precisely,

of time. If I know that, how can I not know what time is? Do I know it, but do not know how to put it into words? 'Nor am I deceptive in this before you,' as you know, my God. I speak straight from my heart. It is you who 'will bring light to my lamp,' Lord my God, who 'will bring bright light into my darkness.'

33. Does my soul not bring true testimony to you, testifying that I measure time in fact—even if that means, Lord my God, that I measure without knowing what I measure? I measure the motion of physical objects. Can that be measuring time? Could I measure the motion of an object, its duration in passage from one point to another, except by measuring the time in which the motion occurs? But how do I measure the time itself? Do I measure longer times by shorter ones, as we measure a beam by a foot ruler? That is apparently how we measure the expanse of a long syllable, by the expanse of a short one, saying that it is, say, double the short one's length. And so we measure the length of a poem by the number of its verses, of its verses by its feet, its feet by its syllables, and its syllables (as short or long) by their length. This is not counting pages, which allows you to find places in a text. But when a text is being spoken, we say that this is a long poem because it has so many verses, with long verses because they have so many feet, and long feet because they have so many syllables, and each syllable counted long if it lasts twice what a short one does.

But this cannot be the only way to measure passing time,

since a short verse can fill out a greater length of time if it is pronounced slowly, as a long one can be pronounced rapidly—and so with a poem, a foot, a syllable. This leads me to think that time is nothing but a reaching out in opposite directions. A reaching out of what I am not sure, but I suspect it may be of the mind. What precisely am I measuring, I ask of you, Lord, when I say vaguely that a thing is long or more specifically that it is twice as long as something else? I am measuring time, that I recognize, but I am not measuring the future, which is not yet; nor the present, which is spread across no length; nor the past, which no longer is. What am I measuring, then—present time, not the past? That was my preliminary position.

34. Do not, my mind, waver here, but keep stoutly at it. God will help—he made us, not we him. Keep at it, there is a hint of some truth dawning. Put it this way: Somebody emits a sound, the sound continues—continues—and then stops. Now there is silence, the sound has stopped, it is no more. It was in the future before it began to sound, and could not be measured because it was not yet. And now it cannot be measured because it is no more. It could only be measured while it was sounding, which is the only time it actually existed. But there was no resting point even then. It was in process of going by. Did that make it any more measurable? Is it the process by which it reaches over some length of time that we measure, rather than the actual present, which has no length?

Say that it is. Then what of this? Another sound begins, it goes on continuously sounding—we must measure it while it is uninterrupted, since it will no longer exist once it has stopped and no longer exists. We must measure while it is still sounding and say how long it lasts. But how can we say that, when the duration cannot be defined except from the beginning to the end. That is what we measure—the length of time from start to finish. So a sound that has not finished cannot be measured, making us able to say how long or short it was, whether equal to some other time, or twice or triple as long, and so on. But once it is finished, it will already no longer be—and what basis have we for measuring it then? We do measure time—but not, clearly, things which do not yet exist, or have no length, or no longer exist, or have no finish. Which means that we cannot be measuring the future, the present, the past, or the mere duration when we measure time—which is, nonetheless, a thing we do.

35.   The hymn line [of Ambrose] *Deus Creator Omnium* has eight syllables, alternating long and short ones, the odd-numbered ones short, the even-numbered long, and the long ones take twice the time to pronounce as the short ones. I recite the line, and repeat it, and find this true, tested by the senses [which sound it and which hear it]. The actual soundings make it clear that I measure each long syllable by a short one, and find it twice the length. But since they sound one after another, first the short, then the long, how did I retain the short in order to apply it as a measure to the long, to establish that the latter has twice the duration of the former, when the short has to stop sounding before the long can begin? And while the long one is sounding, how can I measure that until it stops? But once it stops, it is in the past. So what is being measured? With what is

it being measured? Where has the short one gone, and where the long? While the long is sounding to be measured, where is the short by which I measure? Both have been sounded, have flown off, they are in the past, and do not exist. Nonetheless I do measure, I can confidently say, as far as my trained senses can be relied on, that the long syllables take twice the length of time to pronounce as the short ones. I could not do this *unless* the syllables had been sounded out and ended. So those ended sounds are not themselves being measured, but something in my mind that they left behind them that is still there.

36. So time is measured, my mind, in you. Raise no clamor against me—I mean against yourself—out of your jostling reactions. I measure time in you, I tell you, *because* I measure the reactions that things caused in you by their passage, reactions that remain when the things that occasioned them have passed on. I measure such reactions when I measure time. Time has to be these reactions for me to be able to measure it. Then how do we measure silence, enabling us to say that a period of silence has lasted as long as a period of sound? The mind must beat out the time taken by the silence as if listening to the sound, in order to establish the relative duration of silence and sound within the time being measured.

For we can run over in our mind poems and verses and speeches without speaking out loud, and can compare the lapse of time with other periods, just as if we were saying the words out loud. Suppose a person wants to give a long speech, and he decides beforehand just how long it should be. He has set the length in silence, and remembers what it should be. Then, once he begins speaking, he speaks on until he reaches the finish he decided on. Well, he does not quite speak on, but has spoken, or is about to speak, those parts of his speech that he has covered or is approaching. The mind reaches at the present to transfer things from the future into the past, what is still to be spoken shrinking as what has been spoken is swelling, until the future is canceled and there is nothing but the past.

37. But how can a future, something which is not yet, be shrunk or canceled? And how can a past, something which is no more, swell up? Only in the mind can this be accomplished, because of three activities there—the acts of anticipating, of reaching at the present transit, and of remembering. What is anticipated passes through what reaches toward it into what is remembered. Who can deny that what is to be is not yet? But what is to be is already in the mind, by anticipation. Who can deny that what has been is no longer? But what has been still is in the mind, by memory. Who can deny that the present has no length, since it passes with no pause? But the mind reaches at a present through which what is not yet runs into what is no longer. Thus a long future time is not really in the future, but is a present anticipation of a long time in the mind. And a long past time is not really in the past, which is no more, but is a present memory of a long time in the mind.

38. Say I am about to recite a psalm I am familiar with. Before I start, my anticipation reaches to include the psalm in its entirety, but as I recite it, my memory reaches to take into the past each thing I shall be cropping from the future; so my soul's life-force reaches in opposite directions—into memory

by what I have just said, into anticipation for what I am about to say—while simultaneously reaching out to the present through which what was future is being shuttled into what is past. As I recite more and more of the psalm, anticipation is reduced in proportion as memory expands, until anticipation is canceled and the completed psalm deposited in memory. And the transition that happens with this psalm occurs also in each of its verses, even in each of its syllables and the same occurs in the larger liturgy of which the psalm may be a part, or in the whole of a man's life, whose parts are his separate acts; or in the whole history of 'the sons of men,' whose parts are all the men there are.

39.   Since 'your pity superintends men's various lives,' behold how my life-force reaches in opposite directions. 'Your right hand has upheld me' in my Lord, the son of man, who mediates between your unity and our multiplicity (for we are multitudinous amid multitudinous things). Through him may I 'lay hold on him who has laid hold on me,' and be gathered out of my useless years by following the One, 'oblivious of the past,' not caring for future things that pass away but 'for things prior to them.' No longer reaching in opposite directions but reaching forward only—not with divided reach but with focused reach—'I seek the prize of your high calling,' where I may 'hear the song of praise' and 'contemplate your delight,' a thing not of the future or the past. But for now 'my years are passing amid sobs,' with only you to solace them, Lord, my everlasting Father. I, however, have been disarticulated into time, I cannot put the times together in my mind, my very

thoughts are shredded, my soul unstrung—till I flow together into you, purified, to melt into the fires of your love.

40. Then shall I 'stand firm in the Lord,' unshakable, 'in my likeness to your truth.' Then will I be no longer be troubled by the gibes of men whose spiritual dropsy makes them thirst for more than they can carry, those who ask what God was doing before he made heaven and earth, or when the whim took him to make something after not having made anything for so long. Grant them, Lord, the gift of reflecting on what they say, to learn that one cannot claim God did not make anything for so long, when there was no time to be long in. To say God did not act for so long is to say that he did nothing for a long [time], but time only began when he did make something. Let them stop talking nonsense and be drawn forward to the prior things, understanding that you are before all times, are of all times the eternal creator, that no times, no creatures, can be eternal with you, even if there are creatures [angels] of a special time.

41. How deeply infolded is your secret wisdom, Lord my God, and how far from it have I been thrust by the impact of my sins! Heal my eyes, to share the joys of your light. Were any mind so fraught with knowledge and foresight as to know everything there ever will be or ever was, just as this one psalm is known to me, it would be a mind of wonders, to stupefy one awed by it. Nothing ever enacted, nothing remaining in future years, would be veiled from it—any more than I forget what I have recited or have still to recite as I go through my psalm. Yet even my knowledge of the psalm is far, far from how you know

everything that has been and will be, you the originator of the universe, and of all bodies and souls within it. Your knowing is deeply, deeply more astonishing, far deeper in its mystery. A person reciting or hearing a familiar psalm has reactions and sensations that are drawn apart as the psalm passes between anticipation of what is still to come and memory of what has past—things impossible to you in an eternity that does not suffer alteration, for you are the eternal creator of all minds. Just as your knowledge of what you would create existed at the origin without any stages of your thinking, so your enactment of what was at the origin, creating heaven and earth, was not drawn apart between successive stages of your action. May the one who knows this testify to who you are, and the one who does not know it testify as well. You are supremely exalted, yet you 'house yourself in the humble person's heart.' For 'the crushed you lift,' and they cannot fall who dwell on your heights.

PART V

List of Basic Terms

bounty (*gratia*) The free (gratuitous) gift of spiritual power that humans need and lack.

drive (*libido*) This is not itself lust or sin, but the basic instinct whose indulgence would become sin.

excite/excitement (*perturbo/perturbatio*) What we commonly call emotions—principally, for Augustine, the feelings singled out by the Stoics (desire, joy, fear, and sorrow)—are active provocations to the soul. They excite a response but they do not of themselves move the soul, which a direct transliteration ("perturbation") would suggest. The soul reacts with an adjustment (*ad-fectio*) of itself toward the provocation. To call this, too, an emotion—"being moved"—would hide the fact that for Augustine the soul is always a self-mover. Its reaction is not the same thing as the excitement, nor is it a mere register of the excitement's impact. See *reaction* below, Introduction 1, and *comm.* on **[22–23]**.

express/expression (*cogito/cogitatio*) Augustine derives his sense of these words from the etymology he gives at **[18]**. He says they come from *cogere*, "to force together." I use "ex-press" as an English equivalent that will allow "press" for *cogo* in supporting passages, suggesting both the play on words and the range of meanings.

pity (*misericordia*) Mercy is too mild for the action of God toward pitiful (*miser*) man.

reaction (*affectio*) This is the soul's action in response to excitement (*perturbatio*).

representation (*imago*) This is the mental registration process that receives experience from the senses. It is not an "image" in the sense of a visual replica, since it re-presents in memory things like boyhood or health. The mind is active in making the representation, not a mere passive recipient of impressions.

rescue (*salus*) Salvation is a rescue of the lost.

symptom (*languor*) *Languor* is a fainting condition, not a moral flaw. But in Augustine it is the weakened aftermath of sin, a symptom of what caused his debility, and the divine physician is called in to address the symptom as part of his curing process.

testify/testimony (*confiteri/confessio*) Augustine testifies not only to his sins but to graces, as the Holy Spirit testifies to God, or as earth's creatures have "testified" (*confessa sunt*) that they did not make themselves **[9]**.

testing (*temptatio*) The trying of the soul is a part of the test that life has become in the wake of original sin.

transgressive knowledge (*curiositas*) This is not "curiosity" in our sense but a perverse form of knowledge exemplified mainly by sadomasochism and occultism. See *comm.* on **[54–57]**.

urge (*concupiscentia*) This is not a sin in itself, but one of the basic urges that must be resisted to avoid sin.